KAR

The Complete Book of
Karate-Do

Dennis Wilton

CROWOOD

First Published in 1998 by
The Crowood Press Ltd
Ramsbury, Marlborough
Wiltshire SN8 2HR

British Library Cataloguing in Publication Data

A catalogue record for this book is available from the British Library.

ISBN 1 86126 112 8

Acknowledgements
The author is grateful to the following people for their help and support during
the preparation of this book: John Loyatt 5th Dan Renshi, 4th Dan Iaido,
3rd Dan Kendo, 3rd Dan Jujitsu, and 1st Dan Judo; Dr S. R. Fee OBE, FRCGP;
my wife J. L. Wilton MA, Cert. Ed., RN, RM, RHV, DN Cert.; Malcom and
Christina Bratt for taking the photographs; Jim Breen, Dept of Digital Systems, Monash
University; and my neighbours, Roger and Elaine Hall, for allowing me to use the privacy
of their garden as a location for the photographs.

Printed in Great Britain by J. W. Arrowsmiths Limited, Bristol

Contents

The Zen Priest and the Coin

I saw a priest handing a man a coin, about an inch and a half in diameter.
It was dull and unpolished, but as the man held it in his fingers
he could feel the impressions on its surface.
He smoothed one side with his thumb, and the face of a demon appeared.
He turned it over and smoothed that side with his thumb,
and the face of a saint appeared.
 'See!' said the priest. 'First you polished one side,
then you polished the other.'
The man looked puzzled, then looked again at both sides of the coin.
'There!' said the priest.
'First you looked at one side, then you looked at the other.'
The priest then took the coin from the man,
'Watch,' he said.
He rolled the coin along the stone floor.
It turned in a half circle, then slowly fell to one side.
The priest turned to the man, and said,
'The space in which the coin rolled is eternity,
and the place where it came to rest is another time.
The coin is a life with two sides, body and spirit.
As you concentrated on polishing one side you could not see the other,
yet both are part of the whole life.
Each time the coin is rolled its direction and destination are different.
Look at the edge of the coin, and when it rolls let your senses roll with it,
for you are that coin about to be rolled through time and space.
Eternity is one, your life is one, yet the two are inseparable,
and time has no consequence.
What we really are we do not see but perceive with our senses,
as when you held the coin between your thumb and finger
you sensed the impressions on its surfaces.
By our senses we learn that we are more than a world,
we are a universe, and by polishing our senses
that universe evolves around our true selves.
It is like a dream, and although reality is different from the dream,
the dream itself makes all things possible.
The secrets of our inner self are not secrets at all,
only the treasures of our spirit obscured by a seeming reality.'

August 1987

Foreword

'Every life is a profession of faith, and exercises inevitable and silent influence,' wrote Amiel in 1852.

This faith is not formal religion but an attitude of mind that governs the way we journey through life. On the way we meet stages which will test our minds. An attitude of humility may serve you well for, as Francis Bacon wrote, ' If a man will begin with certainties, he shall end in doubts but if he will be content to begin with doubts, he shall end in certainties.'

When Dennis Wilton began this book, it was initially to test his own mind. Encouragement from others persuaded him to develop the text, so that this book has become an excellent introduction to the world of karate-do. You will find that training the mind, etiquette, methods of sparring, breathing technique and the grading system are all here.

The illustrated description of eighteen Kata in the latter part of the book forms a reference work in its own right.

It is over twenty-five years ago that I stood in front of Sensei Kanazawa and was awarded a grade and a half. Honour indeed! I remember his teaching well; he was patient, courteous and firm, clear in his message and able to demonstrate exactly what he wanted.

Alexander Pope wrote, 'True ease in writing comes from art, not chance.'

Dennis may not have found the writing easy, but I am glad that he rose to the challenge, for it clearly shows his enjoyment of this art.

I can do no better than quote Samuel Johnson: 'What is written without effort is generally read without pleasure.'

No problem here. Begin.

Alastair Fee BA, BDS (Glas.)

1 About This Book

Although karate-do is a serious activity, for most people it is a hobby to be enjoyed, and, as with all hobbies, when the fun goes out of it the interest is lost. Over the years karate has spread throughout the world and has become a very familiar activity. The misguided notion that it involves heavy workouts, stringent training methods and painful sparring injuries has rightfully passed into history. Presently, participants are more selective, and use karate for fitness, personal development, self-defence, and for the enjoyment of sharing an interest with others. Whilst the need for self-discipline still applies, so also does the need for social intercourse. As a result of training together in a friendly environment, people travel all over the world to participate in this activity, and often form life-long links.

As with all hobbies and interests, the introduction is all-important. A simple, down-to-earth overview will whet the appetite and attract people who have an otherwise passing interest. This book aims to present such an overview, which I hope will be of great value to all students of the art of karate-do.

It would be almost an impossible task to describe in detail each and every technique. Some of them defy explanation, and a true understanding of, and feeling for, karate requires demonstration and good tuition. This is particularly true of *Tai Sabaki*, or body management. The way the body is used to execute a technique is critically important. However, because karate-do is a hobby for many people, remembering techniques, and particularly *Kata* which embody all the techniques, can create a problem. The object of this book it to describe karate-do for students already attending classes, and perhaps for students who have been unavoidably absent from training for some time. The Japanese terms at first sight appear a little daunting, but understanding comes with patience.

The word *Kata* is both singular and plural, and its basic definition is 'formal exercise'. (However, given the nature of karate-do, it would be wise to treat all exercises as formal.) Basically, *Kata* are choreographed sets of movements (techniques) performed in a set sequence. The left, right, forward and return directions used when making these movements are referred to as *Enbusen* and may, depending on the depth of stances, cover an area of 10-15ft (3-4.5m). Each *Kata* may use a different line of movement; all the *Kata* listed in this book start and finish at the same point.

Instructors vary in the degree to which they break down the elements of *Kata* during classes. These can range from a single blocking technique to a complete set of movements. When broken down into single techniques the phase 'one count, one move' is often used. This is probably derived from the number 'one' in Japanese – the *Kata* begins with a command from Sensei in the form of *Ichi*, which is

Japanese for 'one'. The first 'i' is pronounced 'ee', as in 'each', and the second is hardly audible, so the commands sound very much like 'each'. When the *Kata* is performed as a complete set the command is usually *Hajime,* which means 'begin' or 'proceed'. Again, the 'i' is pronounced 'ee'; the last letter is pronounced 'e' as in 'egg'.

The term *Sensei* in its simplest form means 'teacher', and is reserved for instructors at 3rd Dan and above, although it is a name which has been inappropriately applied to any person who instructs. In fact, generally, calling an instructor Sensei is a mark of respect and not an entitlement. In a formal setting, such as a Masters course, for example, senior ranks take precedence; an instructor who is usually referred to as Sensei should not be referred to as such in the presence of his or her own Sensei. The rule is that, in any situation, only one person may be called Sensei, and that is the highest-ranking instructor present. When written, the term Sensei follows the person's surname.

The majority of the Japanese terms have been acquired from John Lovatt Sensei, a highly qualified *Budoka:* 5th Dan Karate Renshi, 4th Dan Iaido, 3rd Dan Kendo, 3rd Dan Jujitsu, and 1st Dan Judo. He was introduced to judo during his military service in Germany with the NATO forces. After leaving the forces he became an instructor of judo in a local youth centre run by John Shaw Sensei, and still teaches there some 35 years later. In the early 1960s he became a member of the British Judo Council, training under such notable teachers as Abbe Sensei and Otani Sensei. His interest in karate led him to be one of the first students to join and qualify with Harada Sensei when he arrived in Britain. In 1972 he was co-founder of the Cho to

Ken Budo Renmei and in 1984 joined the International Martial Arts Federation (IMAF) serving as a Director of Karate for Great Britain.

A total of eighteen *Kata* are listed here; many of them have repeated postures and techniques, and vary in different schools as Masters have introduced variations to suit particular purposes. Even within different schools practising the same style variations exist. In most cases, however, the variations are minor. *Shotokan* and *Shotokai* karate, both founded by Master Gichin Funakoshi, the founder of modern-day karate-do, are traditionally equal partners in one style, *Shotokan* being the hard form, and *Shotokai* the soft form. There are many other techniques and variations not listed; they are essential to the repertoire of karate-do, but do not directly relate to the *Kata* in question.

Additionally, *Enbusen,* the directions used when performing *Kata,* are usually described separately. *Taikyoku Shodan, Nidan* and *Sandan* are said to use directions in the form of an 'I', and other *Kata* may use a 'T' shape, and so on. In this book one diagram Fig 18, p.33 is employed which includes all the common directional lines used throughout the *Kata.* Because Kata do not follow the lines precisely, they are meant as indicators only; for example, line 7 means that the action should be directed to the left, when moving forward, and the right when returning. Because line 6 is used in both directions, the letter 'f' or 'r' is used to indicate a 'forward' or 'return' direction respectively.

There are a total of twelve lines in an order that is easy to remember. The numbers ascend from left to right, making it easier to calculate which line is referred to in the description of the *Kata.* If, for example, the description is to face line 8 and execute a side kick with a simultaneous back hand strike, a quick mental reference to the diagram will show exactly in which direction to move.

Kanku Dai requires an extra two lines which are referred to as 'a' and 'b' and are used infrequently. The three *Tekki Kata* are performed in a single line, therefore lines are not referred to. Instead, the direction is either right, left or forward. Looking at the diagram will simplify all of the above points.

To prevent confusion, deliberations on the interpretation of techniques are in separate sections. The interpretations provided are in no way exhaustive. With more research, many other interpretations may be found. However, the value of a technique lies in its application in a certain situation. Similarly, the interpretations themselves must conform to the *Kata* design. With this in mind, to make the *Kata* meaningful, the interpretation assumes an ongoing situation – for example, the action moves swiftly from one attacker to another. Needless to say, *Kata* may be performed purely from a practice point of view by using techniques linked together in a choreographed form without necessarily thinking about the application. From the *Tekki Kata* onwards, no interpretations are offered, largely because of repetition. It becomes obvious after a while that an attacker is coming from this or that direction and must be dealt with, and the techniques needed are listed towards the end. With a little imagination, the unfamiliar techniques arrived at later in the *Kata* will present few problems.

The listing of each *Kata* gives a brief description of the actions required followed by the name of the technique being applied. Checking the list of techniques required for *Kata* will give a more detailed description. This has been done to avoid repetition. For example, *Zenkutsu Dachi* is referred to 118 times, and to offer a description each and every time this technique is used would be superfluous. Once the reference is understood, a brief description serves to jog the memory.

Because of the importance of *Taikyoku Shodan*, and consequently *Taikyoku Nidan* and *Sandan*, this *Kata* is dealt with separately. The *Heian Kata* are described in two parts: a description of the movements, and a basic interpretation of the *Kata*. In the Master Text, *Karate-do Kyohan*, it is said that the *Heian Kata* are so named because when they have been learned the student should feel confident of defending in most situations, and thus foster a 'peaceful mind'. To help with the understanding of these *Kata*, therefore, an interpretation is offered. The techniques required to perform all the *Kata* are listed towards the end, accompanied by a series of photographs. It is worth remembering that the photographs depict techniques as they are performed in *Kata*, but that they may be performed in several other ways. For example, *Uraken* is a back-fist strike that may be used in any direction, but in the photographs it is directed to the front and to the side only.

For the benefit of students new to karate-do, there is a section describing etiquette. Although karate-do can be practised as a repertoire of techniques, it should always be remembered that it is a traditional Japanese art dating back many hundreds of years. Respect for the originators is an essential part of etiquette, as well as being an important part in developing the individual's state of mind.

Included also is *Ten No Kata*, an essential practice often neglected in preferance to sparring. However, inherent in the practice of *Ten No Kata* are the important aspects of 'timing' and 'distance'. Such aspects can only really be developed through training, as with all martial arts, but an understanding of what they are and how they can be achieved is a necessary pre-requisite.

Most instructors design their own syllabus based on experience and tradition. At best these are basic, because success depends on quality rather than content. The syllabus included in this book need not, therefore, be taken too literally. Successful completion of any course requires fulfilment of certain criteria. The syllabus included in this book is offered as a breakdown of those criteria to give the student a framework of reference.

Because the largest part of the text is taken up with the physical structure of *Kata,* a balance has been attempted by adding an essay on the spiritual aspects that underlie all martial arts in the form of *Ki* energy. The acquisition of great numbers of complex *Kata* becomes a feat of memory rather than intelligence. It is hoped that the section on philosophy will act as a reminder of the fact that karate-do is not solely concerned with the application of technique, but can encompass fundamental concepts common to all the religions and philosophies of the word. Although this essay may appear deep and unrelated, its fundamental aim is to show how much can be gained from a personal view by absorbing some of the elusive aspects of the martial art. It is not so much a matter of reading too much into it, as there being a great deal in it which has to be read!

2 The Spirit of Karate-do

UNDERSTANDING KI

Karate comes to us from a foreign country, and references to its theory and practice are couched in a foreign language. Some of the words and terms used have no English equivalent, and one such word is *Ki*. The following is an attempt to highlight this word, and in so doing move away from the idea of conflict towards the traditional aspects of karate. In this approach, there is a relevant emphasis on the spiritual values that owe much to the monks who played an important part in this evolving form.

In the second half of the twentieth century the practice of karate has spread all over the world. The varying standard of instructors and teachers who have transmitted this form has had a significant effect on the way in which the art has been represented. The effectiveness of karate in conflict, picked up by the Samurai warriors, and dissipated throughout the world by a succession of its adherents, has overshadowed the spiritual values perpetuated by the Zen priests.

Sadly, many people see karate purely as a fighting art and media coverage tends to highlight and reinforce the physical nature of this fine form. Indeed, the notion has been fostered that it is possible to kill with a single blow, or to break bones and debilitate people both physically and mentally.

It is an art that can be seen purely in its capacity to destroy human life and, for this reason, it can appeal to a certain type of person who feeds his or her egotism on the ability both to suppress and impress others with well-practised and effective techniques. By such egotism they foster pugilistic ideas, and deprive themselves of the whole world of the true art of karate-do. They fail to distinguish between *Jutsu* and *Do* and perpetuate the idea that karate is for the strong.

However, the reasons why people study martial arts can be as varied as the styles that those arts encompass. While some people thrive on the demanding physical endurance and the contact aspect of the sport, there are many who strive for something more rewarding. They are appalled at the crude aspects of fighting and, while they are prepared to defend themselves by using their skills, they prefer to work towards improving the mind and character and, in so doing, improve the quality of their lives. This was the case with many of the Masters. Their perception and ability was such that some were thought to be unearthly and others divine. Such Masters were not just respected; they were revered. One such Master is Master Funakoshi, the founder of modern-day karate-do.

Can it be said, therefore, that, aside from the obvious physical nature of karate-do, there is a subtle and more spiritual interpretation to be gained? There are exponents of karate-do who would find this unrealistic, believing that *Ki* is a term referring to 'fighting spirit', and that spiritual matters belong solely in the realms of religion and philosophy. There are, however, writers and many Masters who refer to a force beyond the realms of the physical. In his book *Zen in the Martial Arts*, Joe Hymas has described karate-do as 'moving Zen'. Might it be assumed from this that karate-do can act as a catalyst for beliefs and philosophies? In many ways it accommodates the concept of enlightenment inherently expounded by many of the martial arts Masters. One element of karate-do which may be used to illustrate this theory, and which has attracted different interpretations, is *Ki*.

In most respectable karate-do training halls the student is introduced at some stage to *Ki*. To many people, the word *Ki* induces a frown, while others may attach a mystique to it, offering 'lip-service' to something vague and distant; there are some who exchange embraces and hugs in an attempt to pass Ki from one person to another. These different approaches are due to the 'open-ended' nature of the concept, which leaves many people to speculate on its meaning.

One such speculation is that the concept lends itself not only to interpretation but also provides a vehicle of expression. Dr Clive Layton considers in his book *Conversations with Karate Masters* that the word *Ki* – *Chi* in Chinese – may be translated as 'vital energy', but it is a word for which there is no literal English translation. However, *Ki* represents an integral part of all Oriental culture. Dr Layton refers to an authority on *Ki*, Master Koichi

Tohei, who, in his book *Co-ordinating Mind and Body in Daily Life*, describes *Ki* as the 'basic element of the universe from which everything is ultimately composed'. It is said to be the essence of life itself, and can be tapped and expressed through the harmony of mind and body.

In spite of the difficulty in translation, and Master Tohei's description of *Ki*, many people would spurn a Western notion of *Ki* with a connotation of spirit or 'soul'. This is probably because of the strong physical view of karate that many people have, placing their emphasis firmly on the word 'martial'. It may also be due in part to a lack of inclusion of the concept of *Ki* in practice. As Shigeru Egami says in his book *The Heart of Karate-do*, although he had read about vital energy (*Ki*) in books, the subject was not discussed, and this was probably due to the shame of ignorance. He said that trying to find the meaning was like trying to find a needle in a haystack.

There is also a lack of differentiation between karate-jutsu and karate-do. As Master Egami points out in his book, the distinction must be clearly grasped, because karate-jutsu can be conceived as nothing more than the practice of technique for homicidal purposes, and this is most emphatically not the objective of karate-do.

In the same book Egami says that, although many groups trying to understand the soul of the Orient '...in order to counteract the *impasse* arising from materialistic civilization, place emphasis on the spiritual side of karate-do, the sad truth is that many groups teach only the fighting art and neglect the spiritual aspects. And the practitioners themselves, who offer lip-service to the spirit of the art, have as their real objective the winning of matches.' He also reminds the reader that Master Funakoshi himself advocated the spiritual aspects of karate-do, and placed much greater emphasis on this than on the techniques of fighting. 'Those of us who are adhering strictly to orthodox karate as an art of self-defence must do all in our power to see that it is practised in the proper way, and that its spiritual side is understood to its fullest extent.' He says of *Ki* that it '...may be said to be possessed not only by human beings but also by all objects, animate and inanimate. It is said to be the energy that fills the universe. It is desirable to feel the flow of that energy with one's own body. This can be accomplished with practice.'

In spite of this grand notion, the word *Ki*, used boldly in martial arts literature and by practitioners, is relegated to the amorphous role of 'vital energy', or 'spirit', and used descriptively of the moral character of the martial artist. This is a somewhat limited interpretation.

This interpretation does tie in with the *Oxford Dictionary*'s definition of certain words. For example, 'martial' is defined as 'of, suitable for, appropriate to, warfare; militant, ready, eager to fight'. 'Artist' is 'one who makes a skill an art'. 'Vital' is 'of, concerned with, essential to, organic life; essential to existence or to the matter in hand; affecting life, fatal to life or success, etc.'. 'Energy' is 'force, vigour, active operation, power actively exerted'. Although there are other applications for the word 'energy', it is easy to see in this context how the emphasis more frequently falls on physical combat, and *Ki* as an inner reserve of natural energy for that combat. However, if Master Tohei sees *Ki* as the 'basic element of the universe from which

all things are composed', and Master Egami sees *Ki* as the 'energy that fills the universe', might they not be thinking of something of greater significance than human energy and morals?

Moreover, in much of the literature on the martial arts the writers use the word 'spirit' and 'spiritual' in the same context as *Ki*. The more general use and broader definition of the word 'spiritual' is 'of spirit as opposed to matter, of the soul especially as acted upon by God, holy, divine, inspired, concerned with sacred or religious things; ecclesiastical'. Many, however, would speak disparagingly of a Western connotation of 'soul' and 'sacred religious things' as if they cannot be known in relation to *Ki*.

This agnostic attitude would fly in the face of one precept adhered to by one of the great Masters of the martial arts, Master Morihei Ueshiba, the originator of aikido. The precept is that 'martial training is not training that has as its primary purpose the defeating of others, but practice of God's love within ourselves'.

Dr Clive Layton in his book *Mysteries of the Martial Arts* says that Western scientists studying the phenomenon of *Ki* have recognized an analogy between *Ki* and the Spirit of God. Can we therefore concede to a similarity between the Eastern notion of *Ki* and the Western notion of the Holy Spirit and things divine? If this is the case, *Ki* may be understood in metaphysical or cosmic terms.

The Western view of spiritual matters may appear quite different from that adopted by the Japanese, and approaching this problem from a purely Western point of view could lead to a vague interpretation of Japanese culture. A look at history may give a better picture. History shows

15

that, unlike the Chinese, the Japanese have not been given to philosophical speculation. They are traditionally imitative. There is little that is exclusively Japanese. Shinto, their national religion, is a Chinese reading of two characters meaning the 'Way of the Gods' and referred to a superior power, or something awe-inspiring. This is in contrast to the deities worshipped in Buddhism.

In addition to being the moral code of ethics, referred to as *Budo*, the *Do* of karate-do, or 'way', also reflects the *Tao* of Taoism, a Chinese religion and philosophy which became prominent in 453-221BC, later passed through revival stages, and was eventually introduced and absorbed into Japanese culture and religion. The concept of *Tao* was of a silent, motionless source from which all things were derived and to which all things must return. Like the calm before the storm, *Tao* was before creation, filled with mysterious paths not yet trodden and somehow inherent in the substance of all things, the essence of life.

The gods were interpreted as nature spirits. Some were good and others bad, some weak and others strong, and related to something dreadful and awesome or a strange and mysterious power. The strange appearance of objects was considered to reflect the power of the nature spirits. Unfortunately, the powerful philosophy expressed through these nature spirits remained as a seed in the soil of Japanese culture, buried too deep to grow and blossom in the environment of their indigenous emphasis on practicality and realism. They did not pursue the possibility of rationalizing notions of deities and things divine as Western thinkers did; their lack of philosophical speculation did not allow for this. However, Buddhism and the Chinese influence encouraged a more flexible interpretation of the mysterious and imaginary – an integral part of the *Kata* in martial arts.

The superior power of the nature spirits was understood, not by reason, but 'sensed'. This was favourable to the mental *milieu* of the Japanese, and would appear to reflect the notion *Ki*. In Japanese martial arts, the essence of all technique culminates in the power of *Ki* being manifest in the practitioner, extending from the natural form and beyond – the *Ki* of the universe.

Reflecting the ancient Chinese, the Japanese perceived immortality as being physical. The Western notion of spirituality was unknown until they were strongly influenced by Chinese Buddhism. The persistent notion of the mortal becoming immortal is not so far removed from present-day Christianity. Christians are persuaded that three days after Christ's crucifixion his body arose immortal and ascended into Heaven. Can we gather from this that Christ's resurrection was physical? If this is so, can it be conceived that the Japanese spiritual character enveloping Japanese martial arts with an emphasis on *Ki* and the *Ki* of the universe – reflecting the views of Masters Koichi Tohei, Shigeru Egami, Gichin Funakoshi, and others – and the Western view of spirituality, with its emphasis on the universal Spirit of God and things divine, are two sides of the same coin? If so, it would be incorrect to speak disparagingly of the Western connotation of soul and sacred religious things in relation to *Ki* in martial arts training. It would be doing the Japanese a great injustice – belittling their perception of spirituality – to suggest there was no connection between *Ki* and the soul of man.

For much of its history, karate remained, as Genshin Hironishi says in his foreword to Master Funakoshi's book *Karate-do, My Way of Life*, concealed behind thick temple walls. This reflected the stringent lifestyle of its practitioners. Through the influence of Buddhism, many priests used karate as a means of enlightenment, and it was not until the Samurai began to train within the temple compounds that they became aware of karate as a fighting art. Could *Ki* be related to the original practice of karate within the priesthood? And might it be conjectured that when the Samurai adapted karate to their fighting forms that the physical emphasis became pronounced and the philosophy of *Ki* dwarfed? Although the martial arts generally become obscured in the mists of time, are we to assume that Genshin Hironishi recognized karate as the art practised by the monks before it became known to the outside world? If so, the notion of *Ki* must of necessity have deeper roots than we are led to believe.

There are many martial arts Masters who assumed meditation after harsh training. It is known that the pen name of Master Funakoshi himself was derived from his need to meditate among the pines that surrounded his native castle town of Shuri. To the Master, the murmur of this sub-tropical environment was a kind of celestial music. Is it really misleading, therefore, to encourage rather than disparage the Western notion of things divine in relation to *Ki*? The effect of that celestial music might be a figment of imagination, or it might be a link with a divine force. After all, are we not dealing with a phenomenon about which much has yet to be learned? Perhaps we are, as Master Funakoshi says in his book *Karate-do*

Nyumon, '...playing around in the branches of a great tree, without the slightest concept of the trunk'. He says that 'form is emptiness, emptiness is form itself'. This is not an emptiness that means nothing, but characteristically carries the meaning of everything. Although he is talking about karate-do, are we doing him an injustice by limiting the meaning solely to karate-do? Perhaps by edging our minds with definite ideas we lose the flexibility of thought. By discarding the meaningless we encourage the meaningful, and therein lies the form of life itself.

If we continue to use the word *Ki* in its amorphous role as 'vital energy', are we using a word which is basically meaningless, or are we refusing to accept it as the vital clue to the Master's art? Surely this requires more thought, and no philosophy or interpretation should be discarded out of hand.

The fact is that, in spite of the differences that exist between martial arts Masters and their counterparts in religion and philosophy, they search for and express the same basic truth that underlies all human life. For some it is *Ki* or *Chi* extending to a universal energy, for others it is a soul struggling to unite with the Spirit of God, but, as with all intelligent beings, they feel, sense, surmise, and in those activities realize that there is more to life than living.

MIND AND KARATE

To most people karate is an outward demonstration of physical movement and applied technique. Self-defence, physical fitness and sport are prime reasons for studying the art. There is, however, a growing minority that sees karate, along with many other forms of martial arts, as a personal concept of spiritual development. The aim is to challenge the fears and anxieties that permeate everyday life, to overcome phobias and nervousness, and increase perception and self-awareness. To some degree the effectiveness of technique in real terms is inappropriate. The battlefield lies within the mind. The merits of this view are that it helps people to grow as individuals, to develop strong minds, and to fight grief and tragedy in all its forms.

Internalizing an art as complex as karate requires a great deal of thought and discussion. It requires an astonishing degree of concentration and personal application to achieve a mental image of what is usually a silent, unseen pervasive enemy. Stress is a prime example. In various forms it intrudes unknowingly in the lives of most people and is only identified by the symptoms it imposes. It is an internal enemy that must be fought from within. Visualization, a significant feature of karate-do, is of great importance. Individuals who throw darts at photographs of people they dislike are venting inner feelings that cause distress. In reality, many of these feelings hide behind the façade of adulthood and sophistication, and their presence is not realized until unusual behaviour patterns or even illness occurs.

Visualizing stress, loneliness, grief and similar disorienting aspects of the human mind, is a means of manifesting the cause and dealing with it before it has an effect – instead of throwing darts, the hand and feet become defensive weapons. For example, stress might be seen as a malevolent spirit in human form, and, when positioned at every point in the *Kata*, can be overwhelmed. Applying known effective techniques in this sub-conscious manner produces signals in the mind designed to resist and eradicate the harmful effects of malingering disorders – a kind of mind over matter. This, of course, is not a panacea or cure-all, and anyone who has worries about mental health should seek the appropriate advice.

I have already consulted my own doctor, and had various forms of treatment, and I now use this visualization method for combating the effects of spondylosis. Although spondylosis is not a mental illness, it can cause depression due to the restriction it imposes, particularly for someone who participates in the martial arts. Because enemies such as depression are not physical beings, techniques can be executed with maximum intent without reprisal.

The human limb is a marvellous result of evolution, and it only becomes a weapon when directed to do so by the mind. The mind is a power house, capable of emitting tremendous bursts of controlled energy. As Master Funakoshi relates in his book *Karate-do, My Way of Life*, a person can be struck by a certain type of blow and feel very little until some time later, when he may even die as a result of it. I am not alone, therefore, in thinking that the mind can project its power through a strike and its effects may not be known until some time later. Likewise, the effect of striking projected images may be a delayed benefit.

This power of the mind is often referred to as *Ki* energy, and over the years notable karateka have demonstrated it by selectively breaking objects, usually wooden boards. One example is to break the second, third or fourth board out of a stack of five, with the rest remaining intact. Such a feat is the result of many years of training to develop the ability to focus the mind to a single point and deliver the maximum mental energy through a single strike.

These outward and observable feats can be transferred to the inner reserves of the mind to combat fears, phobias and anxieties. I believe that this was the practice of many of the monks in the Buddhist temples. Their lifestyle must have conflicted with their normal human instincts and created varying degrees of mental unrest. It is in these situations that the imagination becomes a very powerful tool. Believing that something is possible is the first essential step to success. By believing that the cause of mental unrest, such as stress, can be projected outward as a sort of 'ghost-like' image, this *Ki* energy may be focused in a very constructive manner. The aim is to strike confidently, to drive this enemy away, and not accept defeat. Adopting this philosophy merges imagination with reality and develops a strong mind.

Our wonderful evolutionary limbs may be used to defend ourselves from without and from within if we use them positively. They are nature's gift and we need no other weapons. In his book, Master Funakoshi recalls that a high-ranking officer said to him 'You know, anyone found carrying a gun or a sword may be arrested for illegal possession of weapons, but with karate the only weapons are the hands and legs, and we can hardly arrest people for carrying those.'

3 Basic Skills and Practices

TRAINING FORMALITIES

Etiquette

Training areas, or *dojo*, differ in size and quality, and varying attitudes among instructors lead to formal and informal approaches to etiquette. Ideally, etiquette should be viewed as being as important as the practice of karate-do itself; it reflects not only a disciplined mind, but also the culture from which karate-do originated. Karate-do is generally accepted as Japanese in character, and the etiquette reflects this country's customs. The beginning of all classes or training sessions should formally begin with etiquette. When entering the class or training area a bow is made. This initially shows respect for the training area and an intention to train conscientiously. It is also at this point that all problems and preoccupation must be placed to one side to clear the mind and prepare it for the instruction and for the practice that is to follow.

The Bow

Although it is possible to write an entire book dealing solely with the proper way to bow, in visual terms very little description is needed. The feet are together, the arms

Fig 1   The bow (side view).

Fig 2   The bow (front view).

to the side of the body, and the bow is made by bending at the waist. The eyes are open, and although the face is directed downwards, the area immediately in front should not be obscured. As with all actions, the bow is an indication of a state of mind. In karate-do, sincerity is the key.

Seiza

Traditionally, at the start of a session, the students line up to one side of the *dojo* with the instructor, or Sensei, facing them at the opposite side. *Seiza* is usually called by the senior grade *Sempai* at the Sensei's

Fig 3   Seiza.

request. Where there is no senior grade present, the Sensei may reluctantly make the call himself. To perform *Seiza*, make a short step back with the left foot, keeping the ball of the foot firmly placed on the floor. Sink down on to the left knee and draw the right foot back in line with the left, keeping the ball of the foot on the floor. Continue lowering the body until almost in contact with the heels, then push the toes backward and sit on the heels. Place the left hand on the left thigh and the right hand on the right thigh allowing the fingers to point inwards slightly. Sit in an upright position with the back straight and eyes directed to a point directly to the front.

Kamiza Ni

The first call in *Seiza* posture is *Kamiza Ni*. The Sensei, who is also in *Seiza*, turns to the opposite (or High Seat) direction while the students remain as they are. On the *Rei* (or bow) command, a bow is made by all. Move the left hand to a few inches in front of the left knee, and the right hand a few in front of the right knee. Bring the first finger of each hand together so the tips are touching. Extend the thumbs and allow the tips to touch. This should create a triangle of space between each hand. Bending at the waist, allow the body to move towards the hands. Pause for a moment, then raise the body, placing the left hand on the left thigh followed by the right hand on the right thigh. In performing this bow, everyone is showing respect to the highest order. For some, this means Master Funakoshi, the founder of modern-day karate, for others it is a known Master, and for others it may even be God, or the divine order of nature.

Fig 4   Kamiza Ni (i).

Fig 5   Kamiza Ni (ii).

Sensei Ni

The next command is *Sensei Ni*. The Sensei turns to face the students and on the *Rei* command a second bow is made, this time to the Sensei. It is an important mark of respect to allow the Sensei to finish his bow before the student rises. If the student has performed *Sensei Rei* correctly he will hardly be aware that the Sensei has returned his courtesy.

Mokuso

In essence, *Mokuso* is meditation while seated in *Seiza*. It may last for several minutes, or for several hours. For the Japanese, the *Seiza*, or kneeling position, may be assumed from an early age. For non-Japanese used to sitting, *Seiza* could present problems, especially if the position

Fig 6   Mokuso (i).

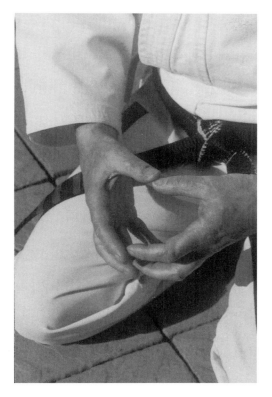

Fig 7   Mokuso (ii).

is required to be kept for any length of time. In karate practice, a minute or so of *Mokuso* may be performed at the beginning of a training session to help clear and focus the mind, or at the end of the practice to help calm the mind and relax the body.

Kihon

Kihon is the formal practice of basic techniques. Under the direction of the Sensei, students cross the hall in a line, executing a pre-determined technique, and are offered guidance and correction. All the basic blocks, stances and kicks, essential for the practice of karate-do, are repeated, examined and constantly revised. The aim is to strive to make the techniques as natural as possible. All bad habits must be eradicated, because what is learned in *Kihon* is obviously transferred to partner work and *Kata;* any inadequate practice will eventually show up later, possibly at a time when the student will have great difficulty changing. Since a large number of students who attain 1st Dan (black belt) go on to instruct other students, getting things right at this stage is all-important.

The degeneration of karate practice in some training situations can be due to ineffective teaching methods, and, in some cases, to the arrogance of students who think that once they have attained 1st Dan they are free to teach what they like. It must be remembered that everyone has a Sensei, and is therefore responsible in maintaining correct practice at all times. The beginning of that responsibility lies with *Kihon* practice. All too often the basics are overlooked when the technical, 'more interesting' techniques come along, because in many cases the techniques are inappropriate to *Kihon* practice.

Bunkai

Bunkai is the application of techniques used in *Kihon* and *Kata*. This is a very important part of karate-do training because all the technical aspects of complex, as well as simple techniques, can be 'worked out' and understood. By learning how techniques work, the value of karate, and consequently its performance, is greatly enhanced. Along with the need for good tuition is the need for a gentle attitude and a trustworthy partner.

The Fist

Making a fist is a very important part of any martial art, and Figs 8-11 show how simple it is to close the hand into a fist shape. What is not seen, however, is how strong or weak the fist is when making a strike. Many students find that when making contact the wrist folds either upwards or downwards, which can be extremely painful if the fist is applied indiscriminately. To make the wrist strong, the thumb and little finger of the closed fist should be pressed towards each other, without altering the shape of the fist. This may prove difficult at the start. The 'unbendable' wrist is a test that will show a successful fist. If a partner takes hold of the lower forearm and fist and manages to bend the wrist, then the technique of squeezing the

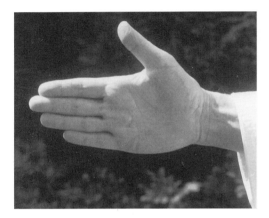

Fig 8   The fist (i).

Fig 10   The fist (iii).

Fig 9   The fist (ii).

Fig 11   The fist (iv).

thumb and little finger towards each other has not been mastered. Only practice will make this clear.

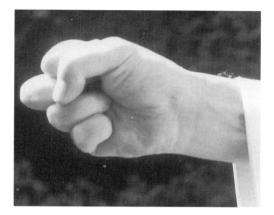

Fig 12   The one-knuckle fist.

A less common fist, although still applying the same principle, is the one-knuckle fist (see Fig 12). Because the shape of the fist is somewhat pointed it can be very penetrating and dangerous. Applied with force, it can produce instant bruising and even split the skin. However, in formal training situations this type of fist can help to focus the mind. It resembles 'pointing' and takes the mind beyond the point of impact, a principle that is applied to all striking techniques.

Striking

Striking can be made more effective by using a technique call *Hikite*. This is sometimes referred to as a 'ripping action' as it involves drawing the arms in opposite directions. For example, while driving forwards with the right fist, the left fist should be drawn to the left hip in rhythm with the strike, and at the same time. Equal power should be directed by each arm. One simple way to achieve this is to imagine that two strikes are being made – one forward strike with the right fist and one rear strike with the left elbow. Combining this technique with a properly formed fist will make for an extremely powerful strike, requiring caution and good timing.

Confirmation

The effectiveness of both striking and blocking is amplified by 'confirming' in the

Industrial rubber bands

Figs 13 & 14 Rubber bands experiment.

Industrial rubber bands

stance. This means that the striking or blocking action is made strong not by simply using the arms, but by using the entire body. Although confirmation is a physical fact, it is understood more by its 'feel', which makes the description of it rather difficult. However, a few simple guidelines followed by practice will help to put things in perspective.

Having firmly grasped the techniques of making the fist and striking, the student now needs to combine these with a positive stance involving a more subtle form of *Hikite*. One experiment I carried out with my own students worked very well. It involved tying together several tough industrial rubber bands 1in (2.5cm) wide, 4in (10cm) in diameter and approximately one-sixteenth of an inch (1.5mm) thick. One end was attached to the wrist of the striking arm and the other end to the ankle of the rear leg; there should be a significant amount of tension when stretched out in the striking posture (see Figs 13 and 14). The principle behind this experiment is to press the rear foot towards the floor while striking forwards with the other fist, simulating the 'ripping' action of *Hikite*. The rubber band idea is simple, but it is a very effective way of achieving confirmation in the stance. Its success relies to a large extent on the tension achieved in the rubber bands when stretched out in a striking posture. Too little or too great a tension will lead to ineffectiveness. The actual strength of the student must also be a consideration. The rubber bands should be gauged to give maximum stretch at the point of impact. Dropping the body weight slightly and focusing the mind forward to a point beyond the target will make this strike very difficult to block.

This experiment worked equally well when fewer rubber bands were attached to each wrist when striking. The *Hikite* principle was more successful when the rubber bands were stretched to capacity. However, the measurement must be designed to bring the non-striking fist to the hip and not to the rear of the body.

BREATHING

Air, like water, is essential to life, but if it is in the wrong place at the wrong time it can be fatal. Ideally, all executed techniques should be accompanied with exhalation. If someone is struck in the solar plexus with air trapped in their lungs, it can be very painful, and disabling. It can lead to difficulty in breathing, with an inability to inhale fully, physical performance would be inefficient, and coughing and vomiting may occur, with the strong possibility of vomit being inhaled. Clinical evidence of shock, including pallor and an increased rate of heartbeat, may persist for some time, and local damage to the upper central abdomen will cause swelling which may take several days to settle down. There is the added danger, particularly after a meal, of superficial damage to the stomach wall itself. For someone suffering with a cardio-vascular disease, the associated pain and breathing difficulty could be quite serious. It is essential, therefore, as with all strenuous physical exercise, that medical advice is sought prior to beginning karate.

It is difficult for many people to comprehend the power that an experienced karateka can generate in one single blow. Years are spent training the mind to focus all the physical and psychological energy to one point of contact. It is extremely rare, however, that such energy is directed towards another human being, because the result would almost certainly be death. Such practitioners are rare indeed. In modern society, few people have the time to dedicate themselves to such training, and, except in times of war, no self-respecting Sensei would teach such methods. Most strikes made by modern practitioners are, therefore, 'average', and the student who observes the important training guidelines will go a long way to avoiding the problems described above. One fundamental guideline is 'exhalation'.

When performing a technique the exhalation is simply continued until, at the point of contact, the lungs are depleted of air. A little practice will make this clear, although too much practice is to be avoided, to prevent giddiness and confusion. Breathe normally for a moment or two then, at random, make one of the exhalations prolonged so that all the air is squeezed out of the lower part of the diaphragm. This causes the rib cage to contract and the muscles around the solar plexus to tighten. With sufficient practice, and well-toned stomach muscles, it is possible to withstand a powerful strike to the solar plexus without 'winding' or injury. Needless to say, this needs to be practised *very carefully, and with good supervision*. Students new to karate practice are not advised to indulge in this practice on their own.

Kata are excellent for practising breathing techniques. Performing them very, very slowly will allow the student to co-ordinate the timing of exhalation with the execution of the technique. With time, a skill is acquired and the performance of the *Kata* becomes extremely invigorating and rewarding.

KARATE FOR ALL

In an ideal training situation, karate-do is a complete defence system. It is a form that can be expressed vigorously with muscularity, or gently with softer flowing movements. Younger people, older people, and women can gain a considerable amount of proficiency without the need for exhaustive 'workouts'. Although fitness results from training, it is incorrect to use the training for fitness. Karate is as much a mind- and character-building process as it is a system of defence. Sadly, some potential students are discouraged by the emphasis on strength and the ability to fight. Karate is *not* fighting! One of the prime motives for learning karate is indeed self-defence, but it is also a beautiful, artistic and very relaxing experience. Women, and people of a gentler nature, can discover inner reserves of energy and strength which, when applied meaningfully, can be just as devastating as the physical strength of the strongest male.

Physical fitness is, therefore, the province of the individual. A few stretching exercises at the beginning of a formal session should be enough to relax the muscles, and a gentle start to *Kihon* should build up to a strong and positive action. Because of individual differences in the make-up of the human body, people respond to exercise in a variety of ways. Ectomorphs are more physically capable of hard strenuous work, whereas endomorphs are more agile and athletic, and the border-line between the two types is ill defined. Introducing a vigorous exercise regime at the start of a formal session can be more harmful than beneficial. Every person has a limit, and the exercise should cease before that limit is reached. The old maxim of 'no pain no gain' is inappropriate. Pain is nature's way of saying that the body is under stress and is a warning, not a goal to be achieved. Training halls should cater for all types, and the session should be an enjoyable experience. If there is a hint of prejudice, bias, abuse or unease, vote with your feet and find another place!

GRADINGS

Belts

The belt system used in karate-do has a variety of colours. Different styles may have different intermediate colours but invariably the belts run from white to black. The reasons why coloured belts are awarded gives rise to a variety of interpretations.

One interpretation sees the symbolism of the novice starting with white to denote the purity of innocence, and returning to white to denote the purity of spirit through dedication in training. As the novice progresses, the belt gets dirtier, passes through various colours of soiling, until the outer surface wears away to reveal the whiteness of the material below.

Another interpretation sees the levels of maturity and rank that the Zen Buddhist priests passed through on their spiritual journey. The novice wore white to denote his joining the priesthood, and returned to white at a senior level of development.

A third interpretation has the belts representing the Eastern notion of reincarnation, passing through cycles of life to reach the final stage of ultimate bliss and purity.

Some think that the belt system was devised in the West as the result of vanity in wanting to show prowess and superiority in competition. It is probable, however, that the colours were derived by accident, since the belt does have the practical purpose of holding the jacket together. Whatever the interpretation, the coloured belts are sought after both in the West and in the East, and the most coveted of all is the black belt. The belts are issued by the organization to which the student belongs for achievement through training.

The Licence

A licence is issued to all students and instructors who have satisfactorily passed a grading test. Organizations have different rules, but all insist on the satisfaction of set requirements. Modern-day karate-do is of Japanese origin, and officially registered organizations have their headquarters in Japan, and are bound by Japanese rules, usually in the form of a European representation. The aim must be for all instructors to be qualified to NVQ level, or properly registered with a bone fide organization. Recently, qualified instruction has become necessary to combat the numbers of unqualified instructors acting independently and poorly representing this historic art form. Any owner offering premises for karate-do training purposes should check the credentials of the person applying to use the premises. This way, they would be supporting a genuine interest in karate-do, and helping to dissuade unqualified people and possibly dangerous practices.

Grading Etiquette

Gradings are assessment procedures designed to determine the students' ability. Students attending gradings are expected to perform techniques and *Kata* relevant to the level of their training, and, on

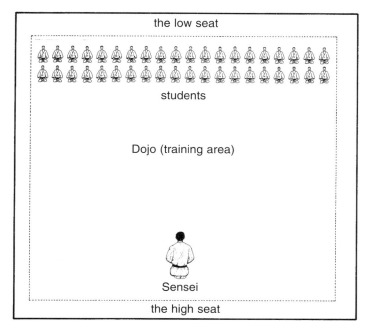

the low seat

students

Dojo (training area)

Sensei

the high seat

Fig 15   In this diagram the students sit in Seiza. This is a formal start to the training session.

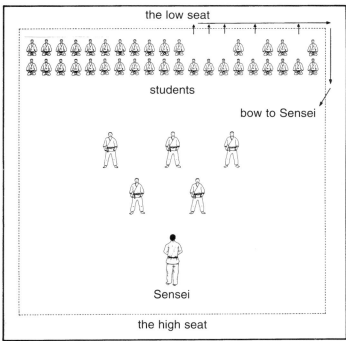

the low seat

students

bow to Sensei

Sensei

the high seat

Fig 16   Grading.

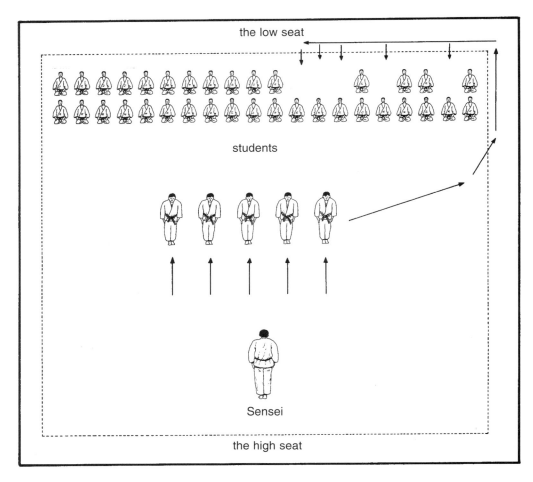

the low seat

students

Sensei

the high seat

Fig 17   Having carried out Sensei's instructions the students step back, bow and resume Seize.

successful completion, will be deemed to have reached a certain level of competence, and allowed to wear a corresponding coloured belt. Clubs and styles vary in the number and order of the coloured belts, but usually they run from white to black.

Competitive organizations award coloured belts on the basis of winning matches. These can range from club matches to national, international and world tournaments.

Non-competitive organizations base assessment on quality of performance and effectiveness of technique. Progress relies more on developing the mind, spirit and character. The aim becomes one of self-competition, in the sense that each performance needs to be better than the last in order to reach a personal best. Through training and good tuition, the students become aware of an ever-increasing demand on the standard of performance, and a greater understanding of the Master's art.

Traditionally, grading procedures express a slightly different etiquette. Although the class begins as normal, at the start of the grading, all students assume a *Seiza* posture in a line to one side of the *dojo*.

In large classes, groups of students are called out by name; usually, students attending for similar rank, for example, lower, middle or higher grades, are grouped separately. One exception to this rule is students attending for a black belt, or 1st Dan. These students are usually positioned behind the lower grades, and complete every request made by the grading officer.

Although grading officers design their own curriculum based on tradition and experience, the grades are awarded on the basis of performance. For example, it is better to perform three *Kata* well than six *Kata* badly. Although a certain number of *Kata* and techniques are required to qualify, simply fulfilling the required syllabus is insufficient. Quality of performance is all-important.

When called, the named students stand, walk behind the remaining students to the far end of the *dojo*, bow to the Sensei or grading officer, step forward to a suitable position on the floor, and stand in a relaxed posture awaiting instruction. These instructions will be called out clearly by the grading officer, and the students are expected to complete them all.

Having completed a set of instructions, the students are asked to resume the *Seiza* posture in the line-up. They bow, take two or three steps backwards, then, turning, walk to the far end of the *dojo*, walk behind the seated students and resume their original *Seiza* place in the line up.

The practice of taking two or three steps backwards before returning to the *Seiza* posture after completion of the required tasks is partly to show respect. It also shows an appreciation of the fact that turning your back to the enemy too soon could be fatal. Although the grading takes place in a friendly, if somewhat nerve-wracking situation, it should never be forgotten that the training has its roots in preparation for a real attack.

At the end of the grading session, the student's name is called out and, after he or she has stood and assumed a relaxed posture, the grade is awarded. When the grade has been received, the student bows, and resumes a posture.

In large classes, when students from other clubs are attending grading sessions, the performance will be intense and formal. Because their overall practice may not be known to the grading officer concerned, they will be asked to perform all the tasks required by the syllabus. One exception to this is someone attending for a black belt. In this case the grading officer may request to see the students at several classes prior to the grading in order to assess suitability for this important grade.

Many students, when they have achieved a black belt, go on to open a club and begin instructing others. Although they may be good at what they do, teaching others to do the same can be extremely difficult. Because of this, qualifying conditions for the black belt are stringent. It is essential that the black belt is awarded only to those who possess the necessary qualities. Since any student who has been granted an award indirectly becomes an ambassador of the chosen style, it is essential that the grading officer is certain of the student's ability. Gradings, therefore, are an important mark of distinction.

When the grading officer is grading his own students, the session is less formal, and the grade is awarded mostly on overall assessment. If the class is small, all the students may be requested to perform at the same time, and the lower grades are asked to leave the floor as the limit to their practice is reached. In these situations, from the grading officer's point of view, the grading should really be a formality. However, the student can never make this assumption, and must perform the required tasks sincerely. An inadequate or insincere performance should lead to failure.

After the grading, the grading officer records all the grades awarded and sends them to headquarters to be officially registered. A licence is then returned, with the student's grade recorded and stamped, and issued to the student as evidence of achievement. The licence and grades awarded will remain valid for as long as the membership is kept up to date.

Invariably, in addition to the membership fee, a charge is made to each student applying for a grade. Business-minded organizers tend to levy high charges for coloured belts, and even higher charges for the black belt. Non-profit making organizations usually levy nominal charges which are used to cover sundry costs.

4 Taikyoku Shodan, Nidan and Sandan

INTRODUCTION

Kata are like scaffolding around the ancient building of karate – all the bits and pieces that go to form the construction of the art, each part serving its own special function. By preserving this ancient form and endeavouring to understand its purpose, like archaeologists, we rediscover the genius of the masters who built this ancient building. As with all ancient buildings, passing time, and often neglect, have resulted in depreciation. The duty of the student, or restorer, is to preserve the original and avoid the temptation to impose an attractive façade.

Master Funakoshi's book *Karate-Do Kyohan* presents a ready-made scaffold – ascending pathways that not only inspire and guide us, but also provide us with an

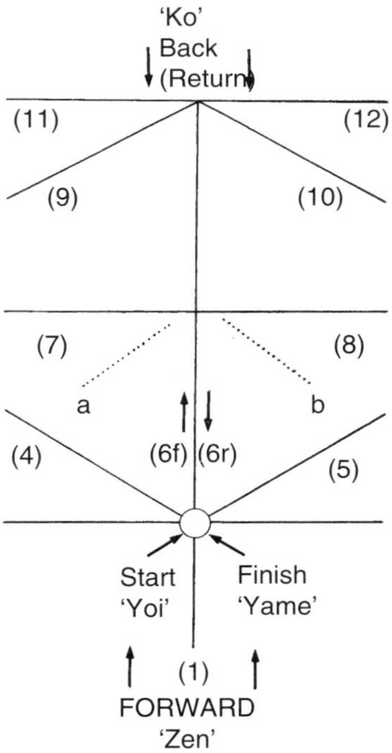

Fig 18 Direction lines used in Kata Enbusen.

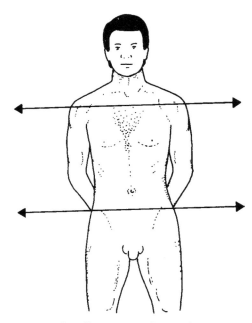

Fig 19 The illustration shows the sections of the body referred to in kata.

overview for our work to come. *Karate-Do Kyohan* is a legacy not only of a true martial artist, but also of a great man with a profound and enduring philosophy.

As a schoolteacher and scholar, the Master could well have written about each *Kata* at great length, giving detailed descriptions of form, posture and technique. However, his intelligent insight in the preparation of his work presents an exciting opportunity to study the depths of this ancient building: a small doorway through which we may '...go deeply inward'. And, one might add, having gone 'deeply inward', find another small doorway through which we may 'go deeply inward...'.

In *Karate-Do Kyohan*, the Master says of *Taikyoku Shodan* that 'Because of its simplicity, the *Kata* is easily learned by beginners. Nevertheless, as its name implies, this form is of the most profound character, and one to which, upon mastery of the art of Karate, an expert will return and select it as the ultimate training *Kata*.' Opening the small doorway of this *Kata*, and attempting to 'go deeply inward', leads to an understanding of why it is an ultimate training *Kata*.

The complexity and variations in the other *Kata* are attractive and synonymous with progress. For example, the student needs to learn and execute well a number of *Kata* to qualify for the black belt – the ambition of most karate students. However, performing well and understanding the *Kata* are two separate entities. The former needs practice and the latter needs insight. Having trained under the guidance of a good teacher, and studied Master Funakoshi's description in *Karate-Do Kyohan*, the student must try to develop this insight and begin his or her own restoration work.

The Master says: 'In all *Budo*, and not just karate, interpretations of the art by those who are training differ to the interpretations of their instructors. Moreover it goes without saying that variations in expression are characteristic of each individual.' It can be said, therefore, that no one interpretation is sufficient, and by going through that 'small doorway' each student will find his own points to add to his personal discovery.

Insight into *Kata* can only be gained by analysis of its form, that is, the fundamental elements that give it life and meaning. Posture, focus, technique and the many intricate details that give it its character are the heart of the *Kata*, and the philosophy they encompass reflect its soul. The following is an attempt to touch the heart of *Taikyoku Shodan*. Based on observation and application, it represents part of my own personal discovery. The heights of philosophical understanding are often reached through an analysis of mundane details, and the following is no exception. It is an attempt to understand the foundation upon which one philosophy stands.

An attempt to offer the ultimate interpretation would be unrealistic. Several interpretations offer any student the opportunity of executing the *Kata* in its original format, that is, without changing the pattern and form. My intention is to offer an interpretation which would not only work in a real situation – which is obviously the reason for practising *Kata* in the first instance – but also to test the form and content of the practitioner. Having placed additional attackers with specific functions in *Taikyoku Shodan*, the student should feel stronger and more capable, on completion of the *Kata*, and approach other *Kata* in a more realistic manner.

A DESCRIPTION OF TAIKYOKU SHODAN, NIDAN AND SANDAN

(Because these three *Kata* are very similar, the minor differences are described in bold, followed by the name of the *Kata*.)

Turn to the left, line 2, into a front stance (*Zenkutsu Dachi*), and execute a left low-level block (*Hidari Gedan Barai*). **Turn to the left, line 2, into a back stance, (*Kokutsu Dachi*), and execute a middle low-level block (*Hidari Ude Uke*) – *Taikyoku Sandan*.** Step forward with the right foot, line 2, into a front stance (*Zenkutsu Dachi*), and execute a right middle-level punch (*Migi Chudan Oi Zuki*). Turn 180 degrees clockwise and step with the right foot, line 3, into a front stance (*Zenkutsu Dachi*), and execute a right low-level block (*Migi Gedan Barai*). **Turn 180 degrees clockwise and step with the right foot, line 3, into a back stance (*Kokutsu Dachi*), and execute a right middle-level block (*Migi Ude Uke*) – *Taikyoku Sandan*.** Step forward with the left foot, line 3, into a front stance (*Zenkutsu Dachi*), and execute a left middle-level punch (*Hidari Chudan Oi Zuki*). Turn 45 degrees anti-clockwise and step with the left foot, line 6f, into a front stance (*Zenkutsu Dachi*), and execute a left low-level block (*Hidari Gedan Barai*). Step forward with the right foot, line 6f, into a front stance (*Zenkutsu Dachi*), and execute a right middle-level punch (*Migi Chudan Oi Zuki*). Step forward with the left foot, line 6f, into a front stance (*Zenkutsu Dachi*), and execute a left middle-level punch (*Hidari Chudan Oi Zuki*). Step forward with the right foot, line 6f, into a front stance (*Zenkutsu Dachi*), and execute a right middle-level punch (*Migi Chudan*

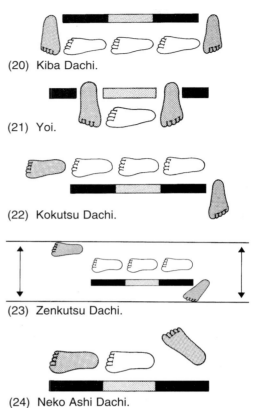

(20) Kiba Dachi.

(21) Yoi.

(22) Kokutsu Dachi.

(23) Zenkutsu Dachi.

(24) Neko Ashi Dachi.

Figs 20–24   Foot positions in stances.

Fig 25   The movements when stepping to the left into a Zenkutsu Dachi (front stance) and making a Gedan Barai (low level block).

35

Oi Zuki). **In *Taikyoku Nidan* these punches are at high level (*Jodan Oi Zuki*).**

Make a three-quarter turn anti-clockwise and step with the left foot, line 12, into a front stance (*Zenkutsu Dachi*), and execute a left low-level block (*Hidari Gedan Barai*). **Make a three-quarter turn anti-clockwise and step with the left foot, line 12, into a back stance (*Kokutsu Dachi*), and execute a middle low-level block (*Hidari Ude Uke*) – *Taikyoku Sandan*.** Step with the right foot, line 12, and execute a right middle-level punch (*Migi Chudan Oi Zuki*). Turn 180 degrees clockwise and step with the right foot, line 11, into a front stance (*Zenkutsu Dachi*), and execute a right low-level block (*Migi Gedan Barai*). **Turn 180 degrees clockwise and step with the left foot, line 11, into a back stance (*Kokutsu Dachi*), and execute a middle low-level block (*Migi Ude Uke*) – *Taikyoku Sandan*.** Step forward with the left foot, line 11, into a front stance (*Zenkutsu Dachi*), and execute a left middle-level punch (*Hidari Chudan Oi Zuki*).

Turn 45 degrees anti-clockwise and step with the left foot, line 6r, into a front stance (*Zenkutsu Dachi*), and execute a left low-level block (*Hidari Gedan Barai*). Step forward with the right foot, line 6r, into a front stance (*Zenkutsu Dachi*), and execute a right middle-level punch (*Migi Chudan Oi Zuki*). Step forward with the left foot, line 6r, into a front stance (*Zenkutsu Dachi*), and execute a left middle-level punch (*Hidari Chudan Oi Zuki*). Step forward with the right foot, line 6r, into a front stance (*Zenkutsu Dachi*), and execute a right middle-level punch (*Migi Chudan Oi Zuki*). **In *Taikyoku Nidan* these punches are at high level (*Jodan Oi Zuki*).**

Make a three-quarter turn anti-clockwise and step with the left foot, line 2, into a front stance (*Zenkutsu Dachi*), and execute a left low-level block (*Hidari Gedan Barai*). **Make a three-quarter turn anti-clockwise and step with the left foot, line 2, into a back stance (*Kokutsu Dachi*), and execute a middle low-level block (*Hidari Ude Uke*) – *Taikyoku Sandan*.** Step forward with the right foot, line 2, into a front stance (*Zenkutsu Dachi*), and execute a right middle-level punch (*Migi Chudan Oi Zuki*). Turn 180 degrees clockwise and step with the right foot, line 3, into a front stance (*Zenkutsu Dachi*), and execute a right low-level block (*Migi Gedan Barai*). **Turn 180 degrees clockwise and step with the left foot, line 3, into a back stance (*Kokutsu Dachi*), and execute a middle low-level block (*Migi Ude Uke*) – *Taikyoku Sandan*.** Step forward with the left foot, line 3, into a front stance (*Zenkutsu Dachi*), and execute a left middle-level punch (*Hidari Chudan Oi Zuki*). Draw the left foot to the right foot and return to *Yoi*.

A BASIC INTERPRETATION OF TAIKYOKU SHODAN

Movement No. 1

Most of the students performing this *Kata* start with a slight swaying movement to the right. They do this by transferring the weight to the right leg in preparation for the first movement of the *Kata*; the step forward is followed by a downward block. However, when they are doing partner work, this rarely happens. On the occasions when it does happen, the timing is delayed and the strike reaches its target without being deflected.

Stepping should be natural, as if you were standing by a bus stop, or looking into a shop window, when someone calls to you from a distance. When you decide to walk towards that person, you do not think about transferring the weight to the right leg, then stepping out to the left: you simply step out. The weight transference is not in the legs but in the hips and abdomen. It is the body that moves and the legs follow naturally. Unlike the step made when walking, which is relatively short, the step made when beginning the *Kata* is a long step into a deep stance. This naturally involves a downward movement as well as a sideways one and creates a spiralling motion. This helps to eradicate the swaying movement at the beginning of the *Kata*.

The Master remarked that partner work was primarily used to improve *Kata* and not the other way around. He says, 'Karate, to the very end, should be practised with *Kata* as the principal method and sparring as a supporting method.' In fact, all the mental concentration and positive physical action required to defend successfully against an attack should be transferred to the *Kata*. This is a little easier when the *Kata* is done quickly, but the impetus is lost when the *Kata* is done slowly. However, the object of doing the *Kata* slowly is to analyse all the elements of form in order to practise correctly without a partner.

Where the defender successfully deflects a strike, the first movement is a positive one, displaying a series of actions happening simultaneously. For example, using the top of the defender's head as point 'A', in the ready position, and as point 'Z' at the end of the attack, and joining all the points from 'A' to 'Z' with a line, the line spirals downward to the left. There is a feeling of gravitating downwards, in a condition of

anticipation. The pressure is released on the left foot, the hips and abdomen directed towards the attacker, the body drives forward, and the movement is confirmed by sinking into a strong posture.

There is no wasted movement in the arms either, such as the left fist being raised to the right shoulder to thrust down into a low-level block. It would appear that the left fist remains at the same point as when beginning the movement, and the spiralling downwards gives the appearance of the left fist rising to the right shoulder. This again could be shown by drawing a corresponding line from 'A' to 'Z' to describe the direction of the fist which is at point 'A' in ready stance and at point 'Z' immediately after the block. The start of the low-level block, therefore, is not at the right shoulder but at the upper chest. To complete this block successfully the left fist does not need to be raised above this point. Failure to achieve a deep stance results in the fist being raised to the shoulder.

Movement No. 2

When trying to continue the second movement of the *Kata*, by stepping through with a front punch, and comparing this to partner work, a difficulty is encountered. Assuming that the attacker has come through with a strong posture, it is hardly likely that one downward block would be sufficient to move the body of the man. The block would only deflect his strike, and this would make it difficult for the defender to step through without a clash of bodies. Although an interpretation can be found to overcome this, the student must not be tempted to change any of the Master's *Kata*.

In this *Kata*, then, we turn to the left,

step into a left stance, perform a down-ward block and step through to make a front strike. By re-examining the first movement, and taking note of the direction of the left foot when stepping through, we find that this can be described as an arc. The average shoulder width – the usual distance between the feet when in front stance – is 18-20in (45-50cm). This means that, when the student is turning to the left to make the first block, the left foot, and therefore the left leg, travel in an arc of roughly the same size.

Furthermore, it can be seen that the right foot of the attacker crosses the line of that arc. This is not often seen during partner work, largely because the defender is facing the attacker. In *Taikyoku Shodan* the attack is obviously coming from the left, and the defender may take advantage of that arc by using the left leg to step to the inside of the attacker's oncoming right leg. This has the effect of disorientating the attacker and making him stumble to his right. This leaves the way clear to step forward, in the second movement, to defend against a second attacker immediately behind the first.

The first two movements of *Taikyoku Shodan*, therefore, may be seen in this instance as defending against two attackers – one making the attack and the other preparing to make an attack, but frustrated by the front punch of the defender. This is only one interpretation. The relevance of any interpretation is that is works well without changing the form of the *Kata*.

Movement No. 3

One point, which rarely shows up in partner work, is the act of turning when defending to the rear. Having completed the second movement of *Taikyoku Shodan*, the student often swings the right leg around in a large arc, presumably to step to the inside of the attacker's oncoming left leg. For this to work, the timing is crucial. Such a swinging movement used against an attacker who has already confirmed in his stance will have the adverse effect of unsettling the defender, and possibly making him stumble. When sweeping the leg around, the balance of the body is not central, with the upper part of the body leaning forward to compensate for the right leg being extended. This can be demonstrated by putting an attacker close to the body of the defender, at the rear, perhaps making a grab to his shoulders or garment, then asking the defender to perform this sweeping action. A high percentage of students will fail to make the turn without altering the body posture at the beginning, and changing the sweeping action to that of a rear stepping movement.

Discussing methods of practice in *Karate-Do Kyohan*, the Master refers to the importance of imagining and escaping from grasping techniques. Placing these extra attackers in *Taikyoku Shodan* gives the student an opportunity to do this, at the same time improving co-ordination and posture. When performing the third movement, the object is to achieve the same blocking action with the right leg and arm as in the first movement of the *Kata*. To do this the defender needs to push the whole body backwards over the left leg, and drive his back into the chest and abdomen of the third attacker, immediately behind him. When successfully practised this gives the defender a good feeling of stability, because not only is this a strong bodily movement, it also brings the balance of the body to centre and gives the defender the ability to drive with the left leg to make his defensive action against the fourth attacker.

Movement No. 4

On completion of the third movement of the *Kata* the attacker should be sufficiently displaced to make way for the fourth movement – stepping through with a front punch to the fourth attacker as described in Movement No. 2.

Movement No. 5

All movements are easier to appreciate when demonstrated than when read about, and much of what follows is a reflection of what has been covered so far. In the next movement, it might be assumed that there is an attacker immediately behind the defender and, reflecting the turn from Movement No. 2 to Movement No. 3, the defender needs to push the whole body backwards over the right leg, and drive his back into the chest and abdomen of the fifth attacker, immediately behind him, who is trying to effect a grabbing action. After displacing the fifth attacker, the defender continues the *Kata* by making a quarter turn, and, as at the beginning of the *Kata*, stepping to the inside of the next attacker's right leg and simultaneously executing a low-level block, and disorientating him.

Movements Nos. 6, 7 and 8

At this point in the *Kata* there are three steps forward, and many students develop peculiar habits when making them. For example, there is often a slight backward rocking motion immediately after one strike, as if trying to gain momentum to make the next strike. One useful interpretation for this area of the *Kata* is that of the attacker, having sensed his vulnerability, stepping backward, and to some extent absorbing the defender's initial block and advancing strikes. However, it is assumed, by the attacker's disorientation, that the defender's timing is sufficient to give him the edge and that he is gaining ground on the attacker. Finally, by the end of the sequence, the defender has progressed to the point where his last strike is effective and it is delivered with a piercing shout (*Kiai*).

Unfortunately, because of this interpretation the first two strikes are often delivered in a non-committed way, on the assumption that it is the third strike that finishes the attacker. In martial arts training, nothing should be assumed, since in reality anything could happen. The idea of *Kata* practice is to devise a situation in which a real sequence of events may take place, so the practitioner can condition himself in preparation for them. When performing these three steps, therefore, the defender should have a serious intention with each strike. The first one may well be the finishing blow. Also, when the third strike is delivered the defender's attention is often focused on the next turning movement, with the right foot pointing to the left in preparation for that turn. This indicates that the third strike is not delivered with maximum intent and this is a weakness that needs to be overcome.

Weaknesses of this sort reveal the mind of the student, showing to all who see them, including the attacker, that the mind is elsewhere and not intent on what the student is doing. The focus of the mind is probably the single most important part of practice. If any assumption is to be made, it must be that the opponent at each point of the *Kata* is intent on causing injury, maiming, or death. In dangerous situations the attacker may be a youth testing his manhood, or a psychotic hell-bent on destruction. This is not always apparent at first sight, and the student should never be over-confident. In *Kata*, therefore, the mind must be focused intently on what is happening, as if practising for real. This strong, positive attitude will become evident in *Kata* practice, and weaknesses of this sort will tend to disappear.

Movement No. 9

This movement has a three-quarter turn. The attacker here is close to the right of the defender's body and is about to grab the right shoulder or sleeve. The defender again needs to use his body to displace the attacker. This involves driving the hips and abdomen backwards while making a three-quarter turn. This makes the turn very strong and positive, and while displacing this attacker, the firm stance resulting from driving through with the hips and abdomen will also displace the next attacker. This is reflected in the first movement of the *Kata*.

The Remaining Movements

Bearing in mind the difference in direction, the remaining movements of the *Kata* have the same character as Movements 1-9, and so on, to the end of the *Kata*.

No one can truly say that they have mastered a *Kata*, because each time the student goes through that small doorway he or she goes even more 'deeply inward'. By going beyond mere training, to plummet the depths of interpretation and meaning, we all take great strides in our own personal development. As the Master says, 'Techniques exist for the man. At the very least, karate training is an endeavour in continued self-improvement.' He also says that 'emphasis is placed on the development of the mind rather than on technique'. This sort of statement leads to a completely different concept, and turns the light towards the philosophical base upon which the foundations of all martial arts are built.

5 Descriptions of the Kata

HEIAN SHODAN

Turning 45 degrees anti-clockwise, step with the left foot, line 2 (*Zenkutsu Dachi*). While drawing the right fist to the right hip, execute a left low-level block (*Hidari Gedan Barai*). Step with the right foot, line 2 (*Zenkutsu Dachi*). While drawing the left fist to the left hip, execute right forward middle-level punch (*Migi Chudan Oi Zuki*) Turn 180 degrees clockwise, step with the right foot, line 3 (*Zenkutsu Dachi*). While drawing the left fist to the left hip, execute a right low-level block (*Migi Gedan Barai*). Draw the right foot to the left so that the heel of the right foot is in contact with the heel of the left foot to form an 'L' shape (*Reinoji Dachi*). At the same time, draw a circle with the right fist, past the left side of the body and above the head and execute a right high-level hammer-fist strike (*Tetsui Uchi*). At this point the right arm should be straightened and the right fist should be level with the right shoulder. Step with the left foot, line 3 (*Zenkutsu Dachi*). While drawing the right fist to the right hip, execute a left middle-level punch (*Hidari Chudan Oi Zuki*).

Turn 45 degrees anti-clockwise, step with the left foot, line 6f (*Zenkutsu Dachi*). While drawing the right fist to the right hip, execute a left low-level block (*Hidari Gedan Barai*), then open the hand and sweep it across the body and above the head and execute a left high-level open-handed covering action. Step with the right foot, line 6f (*Zenkutsu Dachi*). While drawing the left hand to the left hip, execute a right fist high-level block (*Migi Age Uke*). Open the right hand, and, while drawing the right hand to right hip, step with the left foot, line 6f (*Zenkutsu Dachi*), and at the same time execute a left high-level block (*Hidari Age Uke*). Open the left hand and, while drawing the left hand to the left hip, step with the right foot, line 6f (*Zenkutsu Dachi*), and at the same time execute a right high-level block (*Migi Age Uke*).

Make a three-quarter turn anti-clockwise, and step with the left foot, line 12 (*Zenkutsu Dachi*). At the same time execute a left low-level block (*Hidari Gedan Barai*). Step with the right foot, line 12 (*Zenkutsu Dachi*), and at the same time execute a right middle-level strike (*Migi Chudan Oi Zuki*). Turn 180 degrees clockwise, line 11 (*Zenkutsu Dachi*), and at the same time execute a right low-level block (*Migi Gedan Barai*). Step with the left foot, line 11 (*Zenkutsu Dachi*), and at the same time execute a left middle-level strike (*Hidari Chudan Oi Zuki*).

Turn 45 degrees anti-clockwise, line 6r (*Zenkutsu Dachi*), and at the same time execute a left low-level block (*Hidari Gedan Barai*). Step with the right foot, line 6r (*Zenkutsu Dachi*), and at the same time execute a right forward punch (*Migi Oi Zuki*). Step with the left foot, line 6r (*Zenkutsu Dachi*), and at the same time execute a left forward punch (*Hidari Oi*

Zuki). Step with the right foot, line 6r (*Zenkutsu Dachi*), and at the same time execute a right forward punch (*Migi Oi Zuki*).

Make a three-quarter turn anti-clockwise, step with the left foot, line 2 (*Kokutsu Dachi*), and at the same time execute a left middle-level knife-hand block (*Hidari Chudan Shuto Uke*). Step diagonally with the right foot, line 4 (*Kokutsu Dachi*), and at the same time execute a right middle-level knife-hand block (*Migi Chudan Shuto Uke*). Turn clockwise and step with the right foot, line 3 (*Kokutsu Dachi*), and at the same time execute a right middle-level knife-hand block (*Migi Chudan Shuto Uke*). Step diagonally with the left foot, line 5 (*Kokutsu Dachi*), and at the same time execute a left middle-level knife-hand block (*Hidari Chudan Shuto Uke*). Draw the left foot to the right foot and return to *Yoi*.

A BASIC INTERPRETATION OF HEIAN SHODAN

This *Kata* starts with a low-level attack from the left. The defender steps into the oncoming right leg of the attacker, causing unsteadiness, and performs a left-arm low-level block to the attacker's right arm strike. Having unbalanced the attacker, the defender steps in with a right middle-level fist strike, trapping the air in the lower part of the attacker's lungs and causing a fall. Another low-level attack is made to the defender's rear. Turning, the defender steps into the oncoming left leg of the attacker, causing unsteadiness, and performs a right-arm low-level block to the attacker's right arm strike. Having unbalanced the attacker, a grab is made to the defender's right arm or sleeve. Drawing

back with the right foot, the defender draws the right arm away from the attacker, and swings the right arm around, striking the attacker's head with a hammer fist. This causes the attacker to stumble and feel faint, leaving the defender to step in with a middle-level strike and ward off the attacker.

Seeing the defender's left side exposed, a low-level attack is made. The defender makes a 45-degree turn, and blocks the attack, which is followed immediately by a high-level attack. The defender, from the low-level blocking position, opens the hand, scoops around to the right of the body and up above the head to perform a left open-handed high-level block.

At this point the defender has taken the initiative away from the attacker, who, feeling vulnerable, steps back while making a high-level strike. The defender steps with the attacker, slightly shortening the distance between them and executes a right high-level block. While in this position, the defender opens the hand. The intention here is to grasp the attacker's raised arm and, while pulling the arm downwards, drive the defender's rising arm into it. Depending on the force applied, the attacker's arm could be very badly damaged. The attacker makes a right high-level fist strike which the defender blocks while pulling the attacker's arm down on to the block. Having one arm damaged in the previous attack, the attacker defiantly steps backwards and makes another high-level strike. The defender, stepping forwards, then makes a powerful strike to the attacker's arm and wards off any further strikes.

The defender then becomes aware of an intended strike to the right of the body. Making a three-quarter turn anti-clockwise, the defender – as at the beginning of the *Kata* – steps into the oncoming right leg, causing unsteadiness, and performs a left-arm low-level block to the attacker's right-arm strike. Having unbalanced the attacker, the defender steps in with a right middle-level fist strike, trapping the air in the lower part of the attacker's lungs and causing a fall. Another low-level attack is made to the defender's rear. Turning, the defender steps into the oncoming left leg of the attacker, causing unsteadiness, and performs a right-arm low-level block to the attacker's left-arm strike. Having unbalanced the attacker, the defender steps in with a left middle-level fist strike, trapping the air in the lower part of the attacker's lungs and causing a fall.

Sensing an attack coming from the left side, the defender turns 45 degrees and executes a low-level block to counter a low-level strike. Because of the defender's good timing, the attacker feels overpowered and begins to back away. The defender, taking the initiative, continues to shorten the distance by stepping in and making a series of strikes: stepping with the right foot, the first strike is a right middle-level punch; stepping with the left foot, the second strike is a left middle-level punch; finally, stepping with the right foot, the third strike is right middle-level punch. At the end of this sequence, the defender has made sufficient ground towards the attacker to make the final strike the most effective, making the attacker fall under the impact and warding off further attacks.

Another attack is made to the defender's chest on the right side. The defender makes a three-quarter turn anti-clockwise and, stepping into a back stance, catches the right leg of the attacker, causing unsteadiness and making the attacker fall inwards. The defender then executes a left

middle-level knife-hand block against a slightly weakened right-hand strike. As the attacker, unbalanced, begins to fall diagonally, the defender steps to the right into a back stance and executes a right middle-level knife-hand strike. A final attack is made to the defender's right chest. Stepping 160 degrees clockwise, and into a back stance, the defender catches the left leg of the attacker, causing unsteadiness and making the attacker fall inwards. The defender then executes a right middle-level knife-hand block against a slightly weakened left-hand strike. As the attacker, unbalanced, begins to fall diagonally, the defender steps to the left into a back stance and executes a left middle-level knife-hand strike.

At the end of this sequence, the defender should be at the finishing point of the *Kata* and assuming a ready posture.

HEIAN NIDAN

Step with the left foot, line 2, into a back stance (*Kokutsu Dachi*). At the same time, raise the left arm out to the left side, with the forearm vertical and the fist clenched (*Hidari Jodan Haiwan Uke*), and draw the right fist to the right temple with the back of the fist protecting the temple (*Migi Ude Soete*). Extend both arms out to either side of the body. Draw the left arm across the chest, with the fist to the right shoulder and the fingers towards the face (*Nagashi Uke*). Drive the right fist under the left arm to make a middle-level strike (*Migi Urazuki*). Change stance (same position) to a front stance (*Zenkutsu Dachi*), and execute a left low-level block (*Hidari Gedan Barai*).

Turn to line 3, and, reflecting the previous sequence, step into a back stance

(*Kokutsu Dachi*). At the same time, raise the right arm out to the right side, with the forearm vertical and the fist clenched (*Migi Jodan Haiwan Uke*), and draw the left fist to the left temple with the back of the fist protecting the temple (*Hidari Ude Soete*). Extend both arms out to either side of the body. Draw the right arm across the chest, with the fist to the left shoulder and the fingers towards the face (*Nagashi Uke*). Drive the left fist under the right arm to make a middle-level strike (*Hidari Urazuki*). Change stance (same position) to a front stance (*Zenkutsu Dachi*), and execute a left low-level block (*Hidari Gedan Barai*).

Looking to line 1, draw the left foot half-way towards the right foot, and the right foot half-way towards the left foot. Raise the right foot to knee height and, while drawing the fists to the left hip (*Koshi Gamae*), execute a right rising side kick (*Migi Yoko Geri Keage*). At the same time, execute a right high-level back-fist strike (*Migi Uraken*).

Before lowering the right foot, look to line 6f, then lower the right foot on to line 1 into a back stance (*Kokutsu Dachi*), and execute a left middle-level knife-hand block (*Hidari Chudan Shuto Uke*). Step with the right foot, line 6f, into a back stance (*Kokutsu Dachi*), and execute a right middle-level knife-hand block (*Migi Chudan Shuto Uke*). Step with the left foot, line 6f, into a back stance (*Kokutsu Dachi*), and execute a left middle-level knife-hand block (*Hidari Shuto Uke*). Press downwards and to the right side of the body with the left palm. Step with the right foot, line 6f (*Migi Zenkutsu Dachi*), and drive the right hand forwards and over the left hand (*Migi Chudan Shihon Nukite*).

Make a three-quarter turn anti-clock-wise, step with the left foot, line 12 (*Kokutsu Dachi*), and at the same time execute a left middle-level knife-hand block (*Hidari Chudan Shuto Uke*). Step diagonally with the right foot, line 10 (*Kokutsu Dachi*), and at the same time execute a right middle-level knife-hand block (*Migi Chudan Shuto Uke*). Turn clockwise and step with the right foot, line 11 (*Kokutsu Dachi*), and at the same time execute a right middle-level knife-hand block (*Migi Chudan Shuto Uke*). Step diagonally with the left foot, line 9 (*Kokutsu Dachi*), and at the same time execute a left middle-level knife-hand block (*Hidari Chudan Shuto Uke*).

Step with the left foot, line 6r, into a front stance (*Zenkutsu Dachi*), and execute a right middle-level block (*Migi Uchi Uke*), and at the same time change the stance to half-facing (*Gyaku Hanmi*). Raise the right foot, line 6r, and perform a right high-level kick (*Migi Mae Geri*), and after the kick step forward with the right foot, line 6r, into a front stance (*Zenkutsu Dachi*). Follow this with a left middle-level reverse punch (*Hidari Chudan Gyaku Zuki*), and then a left middle-level reverse block (*Hidari Uchi Uke*), and at the same time change the stance to half-facing (*Gyaku Hanmi*). Raise the left foot, line 6r, and perform a left high-level kick (*Hidari Mae Geri*), and after the kick step forward with the left foot, line 6r, into a front stance (*Zenkutsu Dachi*). Follow this with a right middle-level reverse punch (*Migi Chudan Gyaku Zuki*). Step with right foot, line 6r, into a front stance (*Zenkutsu Dachi*), and drive forwards with the right forearm supported at the elbow with the left fist (*Migi Chudan Morote Uke*).

Make a three-quarter turn anti-clockwise and step with left foot, line 2, into a front stance (*Zenkutsu Dachi*), and execute a left low-level block (*Hidari Gedan Barai*). Turn the head to face line 4. Open the left hand, sweep it across the body and upwards to just above head height, step with right foot, line 4, into a front stance (*Zenkutsu Dachi*), and execute a right high-level block (*Migi Jodan Age Uke*). Turn clockwise and step with the right foot, line 3, into a front stance (*Zenkutsu Dachi*), and execute a right low-level block (*Migi Gedan Barai*). Turn the head to face line 5. Open the right hand, sweep it across the body and upwards to just above head height, step with the left foot, line 5, into a front stance (*Zenkutsu Dachi*), and execute a left high-level block (*Hidari Jodan Age Uke*). Draw the left foot to the right and return to *Yoi*.

A BASIC INTERPRETATION OF HEIAN NIDAN

At the start of this *Kata*, the attacker is intending to make a high-level strike with the right arm or the right leg. Stepping with the left foot, the defender makes a high-level block. The defender extends the arms to either side of the body. The left hand is used to ward off the attacker while the right is in preparation for a strike. The attacker then makes a second left high-level strike. The defender blocks the strike with the left arm and drives forward with the right fist towards the attacker's left elbow. The defender then changes from a back stance to a front stance and executes a left middle-level punch. At the end of this sequence, the attacker has made two failed fist strikes and has been warded off by the defender's middle-level punch.

The defender anticipates another attacker coming from the right and making the same attempt. The attacker makes a high-level strike with the left arm or the left leg. Changing the stance to a back stance, the defender makes a high-level block. The defender extends the arms to either side of the body. The right hand is used to ward off the attacker while the left is in preparation for a strike. The attacker then makes a second right high-level strike. The defender blocks the strike with the right arm and drives forward with the left fist towards the attacker's left elbow. The defender then changes from a back stance to a front stance and executes a right middle-level punch.

At the end of this sequence, as with the previous sequence, the attacker has made two failed fist strikes and has been warded off by the defender's middle-level punch.

The defender's attention is now drawn to the rear where the attacker is making a left high-level fist strike. The defender blocks the strike with a high-level back-fist strike and, seeing the left side of the attacker exposed, makes a right foot strike to the ribs.

The defender follows the strike by turning to face the opposite direction where another attacker is about to make a middle-level strike, stepping into a back stance, and executing an elbow strike to the falling attacker and simultaneously executing a left knife-hand block to the oncoming attacker. The defender's attention is now focused on the attacker whose strike has just been blocked. Having taken the initiative from the attacker, the defender steps forward and the attacker steps backward. The attacker delivers a left middle-level fist strike, which the defender blocks with a right middle-level knife-hand block. The attacker, still stepping backward, makes a right middle-level fist strike, which the defender blocks with a left middle-level knife-hand block. The attacker tries quickly to make a left middle-level strike. The defender, having gauged the timing, presses the strike away with the left palm and, stepping forward into a front stance, drives a finishing right straight fingers strike to the attacker's sternum.

Seeing the defender's right side exposed, another attacker decides to make a right middle-level fist strike. The defender makes a three-quarter turn anti-clockwise and, stepping into a back stance, catches the right leg of the attacker, causing unsteadiness and making the attacker fall inwards. The defender then executes a left middle-level knife-hand block against a slightly weakened right-hand strike. As the attacker, unbalanced, begins to fall diagonally, the defender steps to the right into a back stance and executes a right middle-level knife-hand strike. Another attack is made from the right to the defender's right chest. Stepping 160 degrees clockwise, and into a back stance, the defender catches the left leg of the attacker, causing unsteadiness making the attacker fall inwards. The defender then executes a right middle-level knife-hand block against a slightly weakened left-hand strike. As the attacker, unbalanced, begins to fall diagonally, the defender steps to the left into a back stance and executes a left middle-level knife-hand strike.

Turning to the left, the defender faces an attacker delivering a left middle-level punch. The defender blocks this with a right middle-level block and, before the attacker can perform another strike, the defender makes a right, forward rising kick to the attacker's lower chest, causing abdominal pain, and quickly follows this with a left middle-level reverse punch.

Having absorbed most of the defender's striking action, the attacker makes a left middle-level strike. In the same manner as before, the defender blocks this with a left middle-level block and, before the attacker can perform another strike, the defender makes a left, forward rising kick to the attacker's lower chest, causing more abdominal pain, and quickly follows this with a right middle-level reverse punch. As the attacker begins to sway backwards, the defender steps in with a two-arm block. (It is interesting to note that the difference between this type of block and a strike made in the same manner is a matter of emphasis. Although the *Kata* is described as having a block here, the movement would remain unchanged, and the *Kata* unaltered, if a strike were made instead.)

An attack is now made to the defender's right side. Making a three-quarter turn anti-clockwise, the defender steps into the oncoming attacker's right leg, causing unsteadiness, and uses a left low-level block to the attacker's right low-level strike. At this point the attacker grasps the defender's left wrist. The defender opens the hand, swings around and in front of the body, and raises the attacker's arm to a high level. Stepping in with the right foot, the defender draws the left arm downwards while raising the right arm to a high-level blocking position. This has the effect of driving into the attacker's arm and causing severe damage.

Another attack is made to the defender's right side. Turning in a clockwise direction, the defender steps into the oncoming attacker's left leg, causing unsteadiness, and uses a right low-level block to the attacker's left low-level strike. At this point the attacker grasps the defender's right wrist. The defender opens the hand, swings around and in front of the body, and raises the attacker's arm to a high-level position. Stepping in with the left foot, the defender draws the right arm downwards while raising the left arm to a high-level blocking position. As before, this has the effect of driving into the attacker's arm and causing severe damage. The defender draws the left foot to the right and returns to *Yoi*.

HEIAN SANDAN

Step with the left foot, line 2, into a back stance (*Kokutsu Dachi*), and execute a left middle-level block (*Hidari Uchi Uke*). Draw the right foot to the left foot, line 2, into an attention stance (*Heisoku Dachi*). With the right arm perform a middle-level block, and, at the same time, with the left arm perform a low-level block (*Kosa Uke*). Immediately afterwards reverse the arms so the left arm performs a middle-level block and the right arm a low-level block (*Kosa Uke*). Turn 180 degrees clockwise. Step with the right foot, line 3, into a back stance (*Kokutsu Dachi*), and execute a right middle-level block (*Migi Uchi Uke*). Draw the left foot to the right foot, line 3, into an attention stance (*Heisoku Dachi*). With the left arm perform a middle-level block and, at the same time, with the right arm perform a low-level block (*Kosa Uke*). Immediately afterwards reverse the arms so the right arm performs a middle-level block and the left arm a low-level block (*Kosa Uke*).

Turn to face line 6f and step with the left foot into a back stance (*Kokutsu Dachi*), and execute a left augmented middle-level block (*Hidari Morote Uke*). While stepping with the right foot on to line 6f, press downwards and to the right

with the left palm (*Hidari Osae Uke*), then, as the right foot steps into the front stance, execute a right spear-hand thrust (*Migi Chudan Shihon Nukite*). Twist the right wrist and body anti-clockwise, and step with the left foot, line 6f, into a horse-riding stance (*Kiba Dachi*). At the same time as the stance is made, draw the right fist to the right hip and execute a left middle-level hammer-fist strike (*Hidari Chudan Tettsui Uchi*). Step with the right foot, line 6f, into a front stance (*Zenkutsu Dachi*), and execute a right middle-level forward punch (*Migi Chudan Oi Zuki*).

Drawing the left foot to the right foot, pivot on the right foot and turn 180 degrees to face line 6r. With both feet together (*Heisoku Dachi*), rest the fists on the hips (*Ryoken Koshi Gamae*). Step around with the right foot, line 6r, and execute a right crescent moon kick (*Migi Mikazuki*). Immediately afterwards, step into a horse-riding stance (*Kiba Dachi*), and execute a right elbow block (*Migi Empi Uke*), then, driving the fist to the right, line 6r, execute a right high-level back-fist strike (*Migi Jodan Uraken Uchi*). Turn 180 degrees, step around with the left foot, line 6r, and execute a left crescent moon kick (*Hidari Mikazuki*). Immediately afterwards, step into a horse-riding stance (*Kiba Dachi*), and execute a left elbow block (*Hidari Empi Uke*), then, driving the fist to the left, line 6r, execute a left high-level back-fist strike (*Hidari Jodan Uraken Uchi*). Turn 180 degrees and, stepping around with the right foot, line 6r, execute a right crescent moon kick (*Migi Mikazuki*). Immediately afterwards, step into a horse-riding stance (*Kiba Dachi*), and execute a right elbow block (*Migi Empi Uke*), then, driving the fist to the right, line 6r, execute a right high-level back-fist strike (*Migi Jodan Uraken Uchi*).

Maintain posture, and drive the right palm out to the right of the body, line 6r, and execute a right middle-level knife-hand block (*Migi Chudan Tate Shuto Uke*). Step with the left foot, line 6r, into a front stance (*Zenkutsu Dachi*), and execute a left forward punch (*Hidari Chudan Oi Zuki*). Draw the right foot in an arc, level with the left foot, so the feet are about 12in (30cm) apart, then, turning 180 degrees anti-clockwise, line 2, step into a horse-riding stance (*Kiba Dachi*). Follow this immediately by driving the right fist upwards and over the left shoulder (*Migi Tate Zuki*) while driving backwards with the left elbow (*Hidari Empi*). Maintain the stance and slide to the right about 5 or 6in (12-15cm) (*Yori Ashi*). Drive the left fist upwards and over the right shoulder (*Hidari Tate Zuki*) while driving backwards with the right elbow (*Migi Empi*). Draw the left foot to the right foot and return to *Yoi*.

A BASIC INTERPRETATION OF HEIAN SANDAN

The aim of this technique is to turn to the left, and, stepping with the left foot, catch the ankle of the oncoming attacker's right leg to cause a fault in the stepping. This initially takes some of the sting out of the oncoming right-fist strike, which the defender blocks with a left middle-level block.

The defender draws the right foot to the left, and with the right arm performing a middle-level block, and, at the same time, the left arm performing a low-level block, the defender has effectively blocked two strikes. Immediately afterwards the defender reverses the arms so the left arm performs a middle-level block and the right arm a low-level block. When thinking in terms of real applications, it would be unfavourable simply to block and move away. Here, then, the attacker may be seen hanging on to the defender's right wrist in the hope of twisting the arm against the joint. By reversing the two blocks, the defender breaks the attacker's grip and strikes the underside of the attacker's arm with a left rising fist. This acts as a deterrent and the form of the *Kata* is left intact.

The defender becomes aware of an impending attack from the rear and turns to face the attacker. The aim here is to turn to face the attacker and, stepping with the right foot, for the defender to catch the ankle of the oncoming attacker's left leg, causing a fault in the stepping. This initially takes some of the sting out of the oncoming left-fist strike, which the defender blocks with a right middle-level block.

The defender draws the left foot to the right foot into an informal attention stance and, with the left arm performing a middle-level block and, at the same time, the right arm performing a low-level block, effectively blocks two strikes. Immediately afterwards the defender reverses the arms so the right arm performs a middle-level block and the left arm a low-level block. The attacker hangs on to the defender's left wrist in the hope of twisting the arm against the joint. By reversing the two blocks, the defender breaks the attacker's grip and strikes the underside of the attacker's arm with a right rising fist. An attacker now comes from the left with a right middle-level fist strike. Stepping with the right foot into a back stance, the defender blocks the strike with a right augmented middle-level block. The attacker then makes a second, left-fist strike. The defender blocks this by pressing downwards and to the right with the left palm. This has the effect of pushing the attacker's fist strike to one side. Then the defender, while stepping with the right foot into a front stance, executes a right spear-hand thrust to the attacker's sternum. (In reality, this technique would require special training to harden the fingers and fingertips in order to inflict any reasonable amount of pain to deter an attacker.) By chance, the attacker, undeterred by the spear-hand strike, has used the left hand to grasp the defender's right wrist. The defender escapes by twisting the right wrist over in an anti-clockwise direction, rotating the body 180 degrees, and steps in with the left foot into a horse-riding stance. At the same time as the stance is confirmed, the defender snatches the right fist to the right hip, and executes a left hammer-fist strike to the lower ribs of the attacker. The attacker, reeling from the strike, steps backwards. The defender steps towards the attacker with the right foot into a front stance and executes a right middle-level forward punch.

At this point there are a number of options open to the defender. Having defeated the attacker, the defender's right arm, already extended from the previous strike, can be driven upwards and around while drawing the feet together in an informal attention stance. Effectively, the driving right arm is directed under the attacker's left armpit and, at the point of turning, an upward circular thrust is made as the right fist is drawn to the right hip. This has the effect of throwing the attacker out of range.

Another option is that, having defeated the previous attacker, the defender becomes aware of the next attacker from the rear, and turns in anticipation, assuming an informal attention stance with the fists on the hips. As the second attacker steps in, the defender, stepping around with the right foot, executes a right crescent moon kick. The aim of the kick is to drive the foot downwards in front of the attacker to slow the approach and, fractionally before the attacker's foot reaches into stance, the defender stamps down with the right foot to the outside of the attacker's leg, causing unsteadiness. As the defender confirms a horse-riding stance, the attacker makes a right-fist strike, which the defender blocks immediately by pivoting at the waist and driving the right elbow across the oncoming strike to deflect it, and follows this with a right back-fist strike to the attacker's upper body.

A similar attack is made from the right, and the defender repeats the defensive moves – turning 180 degrees and, as the attacker steps in, stepping around with the left foot and executing a left crescent moon kick. The aim of the kick is to drive the foot downwards in front of the attacker to slow the approach, and fractionally before the attacker's foot reaches into stance, the defender stamps down with the left foot to the outside of the attacker's leg, causing unsteadiness. As the defender confirms a horse-riding stance, the attacker makes a left-fist strike; the defender blocks it immediately by pivoting at the waist and driving the left elbow across the oncoming strike to deflect it, and follows this with a left back-fist strike to the attacker's upper body.

A similar attack is made from the left, and the defender repeats the defensive moves – turning 180 degrees and, as the attacker steps in, the defender steps around with the right foot and executes a right crescent moon kick. The aim of the kick is to drive the foot downwards in front of the attacker to slow the approach and, fractionally before the attacker's foot reaches into stance, the defender stamps down with the right foot to the outside of the attacker's leg, causing unsteadiness. As the defender confirms a horse-riding stance, the attacker makes a right-fist strike; the defender blocks immediately by pivoting at the waist and driving the right elbow across the oncoming strike to deflect it, and follows this with a right back-fist strike to the attacker's upper body.

At this point it might be assumed that the previous attacker, weakened by the back-fist strike to the upper body, is now very close to the defender. Maintaining the posture, the defender opens the right hand and sweeps forward, pressing against the attacker's chest. As the attacker begins to reel backwards, the defender pushes further by stepping towards the attacker into a front stance, and executes a left middle-level fist punch.

The defender, drawing the right foot in an arc level with the left foot, sees another attacker reaching out to make a grab. Turning 180 degrees anti-clockwise, the defender steps into a horse-riding stance and immediately drives the right fist upwards and over the left shoulder to strike the oncoming attacker to the face. At the same time, the defender drives the left elbow backwards into the attacker's abdomen.

The attacker, having evaded the defender's strikes, has moved slightly to the right. Maintaining the stance, the defender slides to the right about 5 or 6in (12-15cm) and drives the left fist upwards and over the right shoulder, striking the attacker in the face, while, at the same time, driving back-

wards with the right elbow and striking the attacker in the solar plexus. The attackers, defeated, now fall away.

HEIAN YODAN

Step with the left foot, line 2, into a back stance (*Kokutsu Dachi*). Raise the right hand to the right side of the face with the back of the hand resting on the temple, and at the same time raise the left arm out to the left side of the body, bent at the elbow, with the forearm directed upwards, and the thumb edge of the hand directed towards the face (*Kaishu Haiwan Uke*). Maintaining the stance position, turn to face line 3, and move the body weight over the left leg (*Kokutsu Dachi*). Draw the hand downwards and upwards, in a semi-circle, raise the left hand to the left side of the face with the back of the hand resting on the temple, and at the same time raise the right arm out to the right side of the body, bent at the elbow, with the forearm directed upwards, and the thumb edge of the hand directed towards the face (*Kaishu Haiwan Uke*).

Step with the left foot, line 6f, into a front stance (*Zenkutsu Dachi*). At the same time, drive the fists down from the original position, allowing them to cross at the wrist about 6in (15cm) above the left knee (*Gedan Juji Uke*). Step forwards with the right foot, line 6f, into a back stance (*Kokutsu Dachi*), and execute a right-arm middle-level block supported by the left fist at the elbow (*Migi Chudan Morote Uke*). Turn the head to face line 7, and draw the left foot to the right foot into an informal attention stance (*Heisoku Dachi*). Draw the right fist to the right hip and the left fist to rest on top of the right fist with the fingers directed upward (*Koshi*

Gamae). Drive the left leg out to the left side of the body to perform a middle-level foot strike (*Hidari Yoko Geri Keage*) and, at the same time, drive the left arm out to the left side of the body to execute a high-level back-fist strike (*Hidari Uraken Uchi*). After making the foot strike, step with the left leg, line 7, into a front stance (*Zenkutsu Dachi*), then, drawing the right elbow around and in front of the body, strike the left open hand palm with the right elbow (*Migi Mae Empi*).

Reflecting the movements of 6 and 7, turn the head to face line 8, draw the right foot to the left foot into an informal attention stance (*Heisoku Dachi*). Draw the left fist to the left hip and the right fist to rest on top of the left fist with the fingers directed upwards (*Koshi Gamae*). Drive out to the right side of the body to perform a middle-level foot strike (*Migi Yoko Geri Keage*) and, at the same time, drive the right arm out to the right side of the body to execute a high-level back-fist strike (*Migi Uraken Uchi*). After making the foot strike, step with the right leg, line 8, into a front stance (*Zenkutsu Dachi*), then, drawing the left elbow around and in front of the body, strike the right open hand palm with the left elbow (*Hidari Mae Empi*). Maintaining the front stance, turn the head to face line 6f. While drawing the right hand to the right side of the face, sweep the left hand down to a point about 15in (35cm) in front of the left thigh (*Hidari Shuto Gedan Barai*). Maintain the same stance position and, pivoting at the hips, move the body weight over the left leg and reverse the stance (*Hidari Zenkutsu Dachi*). At the same time, draw the back of the left hand to a point just in front of and slightly above the forehead, drive forwards with the right hand to execute a high-level

knife-hand strike (*Migi Shuto Jodan Uke*).

Stepping with the right foot, line 6f, execute a right high-level kick (*Migi Jodan Mae Geri*). After lowering the right foot, draw the left foot to the outside edge of the right foot (*Kosa Dachi*) and, rotating the right arm in a backward circle, strike downwards to a right middle-level back-fist strike (*Migi Chudan Uraken Uchi*), while drawing the left fist to the left hip.

Rotating on the balls of the feet, turn anti-clockwise, and step with the left foot, line 10, into a front stance (*Zenkutsu Dachi*). Drive both open hands forwards, allowing them to cross at the wrists, until they are at about shoulder height (*Jodan Juji Uke*). Move the body weight over the right leg into a back stance (*Kokutsu Dachi*) and, closing the hands, draw the fists apart to perform a double-forearm opening block (*Kakiwake Uchi*). Stepping with the right leg, line 10, execute a right high-level kick (*Migi Jodan Mae Geri*) and, lowering into a right front stance (*Zenkutsu Dachu*), execute a right middle-level punch (*Migi Chudan Oi Zuki*), followed quickly by a left middle-level reverse punch (*Hidari Chudan Gyaku Zuki*). Turn clockwise and step with the right foot, line 9, into a front stance (*Zenkutsu Dachi*). Drive both open hands forwards, allowing them to cross at the wrists, until they are at about shoulder height (*Jodan Juji Uke*). Move the body weight over the left leg into a back stance (*Kokutsu Dachi*) and, closing the hands, draw the fists apart to perform a double-forearm opening block (*Kakiwake Uchi*). Stepping with the left leg, line 9, execute a left high-level kick (*Hidari Jodan Mae Geri*) and, lowering into a right front stance, execute a left middle-level punch (*Hidari Chudan Oi Zuki*), followed quickly by a right middle-level reverse punch (*Migi Chudan Gyaku Zuki*).

Step across with the left foot, line 6r, into a back stance (*Kokutsu Dachi*) and, at the same time, execute a left augmented forearm block (*Hidari Chudan Morote Uke*). Step with the right foot, line 6r, into a back stance (*Kokutsu Dachi*) and, at the same time, execute a right augmented forearm block (*Migi Chudan Morote Uke*). Step with the left foot, line 6r, into a back stance (*Kokutsu Dachi*) and, at the same time, execute a left augmented forearm block (*Hidari Chudan Morote Uke*). Move the body weight forward over the left leg and change to a front stance. At the same time, reach forward with both hands to about head height with the palms facing each other (*Morote Kubi Osae*). Drive upwards with the right knee and draw the hands downwards to either side of the right knee (*Migi Hiza Uchi*).

Turn 180 degrees and step back with the right foot, line 6r, into a back stance (*Kokutsu Dachi*), and execute a left middle-level knife-hand block (*Hidari Chudan Shuto Uke*). Step forward with the right foot, line 6f, into a back stance (*Kokutsu Dachi*), and execute a right middle-level knife-hand block (*Migi Chudan Shuto Uke*). Draw the left foot to the right foot and return to *Yoi*.

A BASIC INTERPRETATION OF HEIAN YODAN

This technique can be interpreted in different ways. With the left hand or arm the defender is blocking a strike, possibly a kick, to the head. The left arm is blocking to the shin, while the left hand, while protecting the temple, is blocking against the foot. When starting the next movement the hands are pushed slightly forward and downward, then swooped across the lower body. By doing this the attacking leg is pushed away and the attacker thrown off balance. Another interpretation is that the strike is a right-fist strike to the head which the defender blocks by using the left hand to the attacker's upper arm, and the right hand to grasp the attacker's wrist. When starting the next movement by sweeping the hands slightly outward and downward, the defender twists the arm against the joint and throws the attacker to the floor.

The same interpretation may be made for this section. However, when the defender throws the attacker to the floor by twisting the arm against the joint, the defender becomes aware of an attack from the front. The attack comes in the form of a low-level kick. When throwing the attacker to the floor, the defender also drives both fists forward, allowing them to cross at the wrists, and blocks the oncoming strike with a two-handed cross block. Immediately after blocking the kick, the defender steps into the attacker and executes an augmented middle-level block. Although this action is referred to as a 'block', it could also be a strike. In keeping with the general interpretation of *Kata*, it is preferable to think of this as a strike rather than simply making a block. By making a middle-level strike, the attacker is deterred from making other attacks.

The defender is now aware of an intended right-fist attack from the left. Adjusting the posture, the defender blocks to the inside of the attacking arm with a back-hand strike, and at the same time executes a left knife-edge foot strike to the attacker's solar plexus. This makes the attacker bow forwards. Taking advantage of the attacker's forward bow, the defender steps in and drives the right elbow around to the attacker's head or face, causing a faint.

The defender is now aware of an intended left-fist attack from the right. Adjusting the posture, the defender blocks to the inside of the attacking arm with a backhand strike, and at the same time executes a right knife-edge foot strike to the attacker's solar plexus. This makes the attacker bow forwards. Taking advantage of the attacker's forward bow, the defender steps in and drives the right elbow around to the attacker's head or face, causing a faint.

Seeing the defender's vulnerable left side, another attacker makes a low-level right kick strike. Maintaining the front stance, the defender sweeps down with the left hand, and deflects the kick. The defender, pivoting at the waist, changes the stance to the opposite leg. The defender then drives forward with a right knife-hand strike to the attacker's neck. This strike compresses the jugular, stopping the flow of blood to the brain, and thus causing a faint. Stepping with the right foot the defender executes a right high-level kick. This throws the attacker's head backwards, leaving the defender to step in and execute a right middle-level back-fist strike.

A grabbing action is now made from the rear. Rotating on the balls of the feet, the defender turns anti-clockwise, and drives both fists forward, allowing them to cross at the wrists, until they are between the grasping arms of the attacker. Moving the body weight over the right leg, the defender draws the fists apart to perform a double-forearm opening block. The moving of the body and the opening of the arms has the effect of drawing the attacker towards the defender. Stepping with the right leg and moving slightly forwards, the defender executes a right high-level kick, making the attacker's head reel backwards.

Lowering into a right front stance, the defender then executes a right middle-level punch, followed quickly by a left middle-level reverse punch. The attacker falls away defeated.

An attack now comes from the left. The defender, stepping across with the left foot, executes a left augmented forearm block. In this action, the attacker feels too close to the defender and takes a step backwards. Stepping with the right foot the defender inches forward and at the same time executes a right augmented forearm block. Still trying to make a safe distance, the attacker steps back again. Stepping with the left foot, the defender executes a left augmented forearm block and has closed the distance. Before the attacker can recuperate, the defender moves the body weight forwards and reaches outwards with both hands to about head height. Grasping at the head or hair, the defender drives upwards with the right knee and draws the attacker's head downwards on to the right knee, stunning the attacker.

The defender, aware of an attack from the rear, turns and steps back with the right foot, driving the right elbow into the stunned attacker to clear the way, and executes a left middle-level knife-hand block to the oncoming attacker. As the attacker withdraws, the defender steps forward and executes a right middle-level knife-hand block to the attacker's upper arm, causing severe pain and deterring further attacks. The defender then draws the left foot to the right foot and returns to *Yoi*.

HEIAN GODAN

Step with the left foot, line 2, into a back stance (*Kokutsu Dachi*), and execute a left middle-level block (*Hidari Chudan Uchi*

Uke). Maintain the stance and, twisting at the waist, execute a right middle-level reverse punch along line 2 (*Migi Chudan Gyaku Zuki*). Draw the right foot to the left foot into an informal attention stance (*Heisoku Dachi*), and draw the left arm across the chest until the fist is level with the right side of the chest, and the forearm about 6in (15cm) away from the chest (*Hidari Kagi Gamae*). Step with the right foot, line 3, into a back stance (*Kokutsu Dachi*), and execute a right middle-level block (*Migi Chudan Uchi Uke*). Maintain the stance and, twisting at the waist, execute a left middle-level reverse punch along line 3 (*Hidari Chudan Gyaku Zuki*). Draw left foot to right foot into an informal attention stance (*Heisoku Dachi*), and draw the right arm across the chest until the fist is level with the left side of the chest, and the forearm about 6in (15cm) away from the chest (*Migi Kagi Gamae*).

Step with the right foot, line 6f, into a back stance (*Kokutsu Dachi*), and, at the same time, execute a right middle-level augmented block (*Migi Chudan Morote Uke*). Step with the left foot, line 6f, into a front stance (*Zenkutsu Dachi*) and, at the same time, drive both arms downwards, allowing them to cross at the wrists, into a low-level blocking position (*Gedan Juji Uke*), then raise the arms, keeping the wrists crossed, and allowing the hands to open, to a high-level blocking position (*Jodan Haishu Juji Uke*). While maintaining contact at the wrists, draw the hands to the right hip, rotating the hands in opposite directions as they are being drawn downwards. Allow the fists to close at the right hip, and immediately afterwards execute a left low-level block (*Hidari Gedan Barai*). Step with the right foot, line 6f, into a front stance (*Zenkutsu Dachi*), and

execute a right middle-level punch (*Migi Chudan Oi Zuki*).

Turn 180 degrees anti-clockwise, line 6r, while executing a right crescent moon kick (*Migi Mikazuki*), and step into a horse-riding stance (*Kiba Dachi*), and immediately afterwards execute a right low-level block along line 6r (*Migi Gedan Barai*). Turn the head 180 degrees to face line 6f. Cross both arms at the chest with the palms directed away from the body on either side, with the emphasis on the left hand, which is then drawn, in an outward circular motion, to line 6f, while drawing the right fist to the right hip (*Hidari Chudan Haishu Uke*). Execute a right crescent moon kick to the left extended open hand (*Migi Mikazuki Geri*), then, while stepping into a horse-riding stance (*Kiba Dachi*), line 6f, strike the extended left open hand with the right elbow (*Migi Mae Empi*). As the right elbow makes the strike, draw the left foot to the outside edge of the right foot, line 6f, into a cross-leg stance (*Kosa Dachi*), then execute a right augmented middle-level block (*Migi Morote Uke*).

Turn 180 degrees, line 6r, and, rotating on the ball of the right foot, slide the left foot out into a relaxed stance (*Shizentai*), and drive the right augmented block upwards in a vertical line (*Koho Tsuki Age*). Leap high into the air, line 6r, and land into a low cross-leg stance (*Kosa Dachi*), and, on landing, drive both arms downwards, allowing then to cross at the wrists, into a low-level blocking position (*Gedan Juji Uke*). Step with right foot, line 6r, into a front stance (*Zenkutsu Dachi*), and execute a right middle-level augmented block (*Migi Chudan Morote Uke*).

Turn 180 degrees anti-clockwise to face line 6f, and step into a back stance

(*Kokutsu Dachi*). Position the left arm in a low-level blocking position, and the right arm in a high-level blocking position, fists closed (*Manji Uke*). Pushing the body weight forward, and without moving the feet, change the stance to a front stance (*Zenkutsu Dachi*). Draw the left open hand to the right shoulder (*Hidari Nagashi Uke*), and drive the right hand forwards to make a low-level palm heel thrust (*Migi Teishu Uchi*). Pushing the body weight backwards, change the stance to a back stance (*Kokutsu Dachi*). Position the left arm in a low-level blocking position, and the right arm in a high-level blocking position, hands open (*Manji Uke*). Draw the left foot to the right foot into an informal attention stance (*Heisoku Dachi*). Pivoting on the balls of the feet, turn the body 180 degrees anti-clockwise, and position the left arm in a low-level blocking position, and the right arm in a high-level blocking position, fists closed (*Manji Gamae*).

Step with the right foot, line 6f, into a back stance (*Kokutsu Dachi*). Position the right arm in a low-level blocking position, and the left arm in a high-level blocking position, hands open (*Manji Uke*). Pushing the body weight forward, and without moving the feet, change the stance to a front stance (*Zenkutsu Dachi*). Draw the right open hand to the left shoulder (*Migi Nagashi Uke*), and drive the left hand forwards to make a low-level palm heel thrust (*Hidari Teishu Uchi*). Pushing the body weight backwards, change the stance to a back stance (*Kokutsu Dachi*). Position the right arm in a low-level blocking position, and the left arm in a high-level blocking position, fists closed (*Manji Uke*). Draw the right foot towards the left foot and return to *Yoi*.

A BASIC INTERPRETATION OF HEIAN GODAN

In this sequence a right-fist attack is made from the left. The defender, stepping into the attack with the left foot, catches the attacker's right oncoming leg, causing unsteadiness. The defender then makes a middle-level block to the attacker's weakened right-fist strike. Twisting at the waist, the defender delivers a middle-level strike to the attacker's solar plexus, making the attacker bow forwards, and deterring further action. As the attacker bows forwards, the defender, drawing the right foot to the left foot, drives the left fist to the attacker's head, causing a faint. A left-fist attack is then made from the right. The defender, stepping into the attack with the right foot, catches the attacker's left oncoming leg, causing unsteadiness. The defender then makes a middle-level block to the attacker's weakened left-fist strike. Twisting at the waist, the defender delivers a middle-level strike to the attacker's solar plexus, making the attacker bow forwards, and deterring further action. As the attacker bows forwards, the defender, drawing the left foot to the right foot, drives the left fist to the attacker's head, causing a faint.

An attacker approaches from the front. The attack is a left middle-level strike that the defender deflects with a right middle-level augmented block, driving the attacker backwards. As the attacker steps backwards, the defender steps in. The attacker makes a right low-level kick quickly followed by a left high-level fist strike. The defender drives both arms downwards, allowing them to cross at the wrist, and blocks the kick, then, raising the open hands, blocks the high-level strike. With the arm raised, the defender traps the attacker's left wrist, then, pressing the palms of the hand against the attacker's wrist, twists the attacker's arm clockwise, pulling forward. The defender then executes a left low-level strike to the attacker's lower body, causing pain, and making the attacker step backwards. The defender follows this by stepping forward and executing a right middle-level strike, driving the attacker away.

A left-fist attack is then made from the rear. The defender, sensing this, turns, and executes a right crescent moon kick to the attacker's left arm, then steps to the inside of the attacker's left leg into a horse-riding stance. As the defender confirms the stance the attacker is made to feel unsteady. At this point the defender makes a low-level blocking action to the attacker's lower left ribs.

A further attack is made from the left. The defender turns, and drives outwards and around in an anti-clockwise direction with the left open hand, and traps the attacker's oncoming right-fist strike. Before the attacker recuperates, the defender drives around with a crescent moon kick in front of the attacker's face into the right arm. As the attacker falls slightly forwards, the defender lowers into a horse-riding stance and drives the right elbow to the attacker's head. As the attacker begins to fall backwards, dazed, the defender drives forward by drawing the left foot to the right foot into a cross-leg stance, and executes a right middle-level augmented block. This effectively stops the attacker falling on to the defender. The attacker, now very dazed, is close to the defender. Turning, and rotating on the ball of the right foot, the defender drives upwards with a right augmented block, striking the attacker under the chin, causing a faint.

An attacker using a stick or pole tries to unbalance the defender by driving into the defender's legs. The defender leaps high into the air and, as the stick or pole passes under the legs, descends, driving downwards with the arms, allowing them to cross at the wrists, on to the attacker's arms, in a low cross-leg stance. The attacker, releasing the stick or pole, tries to escape by stepping backwards. Stepping forwards, the defender executes a right middle-level augmented block to the attacker's sternum.

An attack is then made from the rear. Turning anti-clockwise, the defender steps backwards into a back stance. The defender then positions the left arm in a low-level blocking position, and the right arm in a high-level blocking position, fists closed, in readiness for the attack. The attacker drives forward with a left-fist strike. The defender, pushing the body weight forward, changes the stance to a front stance. Drawing the left open hand to the right shoulder, the defender blocks to the inside of the left oncoming strike. At the same time, the defender drives the right hand forward to make a low-level palm heel thrust. The defender then grasps hold of the attacker's leg or clothing and, pushing the body weight backwards, changes the stance to a back stance, at the same time drawing the right arm in a high-level blocking position and the left arm in a low-level blocking position, fists closed. This effectively pulls the legs from under the attacker, causing a severe fall.

Another attacker drives forwards with a left-foot strike. Making some distance, the defender draws the left foot to the right foot into an informal attention stance, pivots on the balls of feet, and turns 180 degrees anti-clockwise. Stepping with the right foot into a back stance, the defender positions the right arm in a low-level blocking position, and the left arm in a high-level blocking position, hands open. The attacker, having missed with the foot strike, makes a right-fist strike. The defender, pushing the body weight forward, changes to a front stance. Drawing the right fist to the left shoulder, the defender blocks the oncoming strike. At the same time the defender drives the left hand forward to make a low-level palm heel thrust. The defender then grasps hold of the attacker's leg or clothing and, pushing the body weight backward, changes to a back stance, at the same time drawing the right arm in a high-level blocking position and the left arm in a low-level blocking position, fists closed. This effectively pulls the legs from under the attacker, causing a severe fall. The defender draws the right foot towards the left foot and returns to *Yoi*.

TEKKI SHODAN

Stand with the feet together and the hands crossed by the groin. The palm of the right hand is pressed against the back of the left hand, and the hands form an 'X' shape. Look to the right. Step with the left foot over the right foot into a crossed-legs stance (*Kosa Dachi*). Stepping to the right and using the outer edge of the right foot, execute a right rising kick (*Migi Yoko Geri Keage*), then step into a horse-riding stance (*Kiba Dachi*). Draw the left fist to the left hip, and drive around to the right with the right back open hand to a high level (*Migi Jodan Haishu Uke*), then strike the right open palm with the left elbow (*Sokumen Empi*), and draw both fists to the right hip (*Koshi Gamae*).

Look to the left, and drive the left arm down to the left side of the body to a low-level blocking position (*Hidari Gedan Barai*), then, while drawing the left fist to the left hip, drive the right fist across the chest to the left side of the body at middle level (*Migi Kagi Zuki*). Step to the left with the right foot over the left foot into a crossed-legs stance (*Kosa Dachi*), and drive to the left with the outside edge of the left foot to make a middle-level rising kick (*Hidari Yoko Geri Keage*), then step into a horse-riding stance (*Kiba Dachi*).

Look forward and execute a middle-level right forearm block (*Migi Uchi Uke*). Raise the left arm to the left side of the body in an 'L' shape to a high-level blocking position (*Jodan Nagashi Uke*), and the right to a low-level blocking position (*Migi Gedan Barai*), then drive forwards to head height with the left back fist and support the left elbow with the right back fist (*Hidari Jodan Urazuki*).

Maintaining the arm position, look to the left and quickly sweep the left foot up towards the right thigh, then back into stance (*Hidari Nami Ashi*), then drive the supported left arm around to the left side of the body to make a middle-level block (*Sokumen Uke*). Look to the right, and repeat the same action to the right – quickly sweep the right foot upwards towards the left thigh (*Migi Nami Ashi*), then drive the supported left arm around to the right side of the body (*Sokumen Uke*). Looking to the left, draw both fists to the right hip (*Koshi Gamae*), then drive both fists out to the left side of the body (*Morote Zuki*). Drawing the right fist back to the right hip, bring the left open hand close to the abdomen, then drive the back of the hand out to the left side of the body to high level (*Hidari Haishu Uke*), then strike the left open hand with the right elbow (*Sokumen Empi*).

Look to the right and draw both fists to the left hip (*Koshi Gamae*), then drive the right fist downwards to the right side of the body to a low-level blocking position (*Migi Gedan Barai*) and, drawing the right fist to the right hip, drive across the chest with the left fist to middle level (*Hidari Kagi Zuki*).

Step with the left foot over the right foot into a crossed-legs stance (*Kosa Dachi*), and drive outwards to the right with the outside edge of the right foot to make a middle-level rising side kick (*Migi Yoko Geri Keage*), then step into a horse-riding stance (*Kiba Dachi*). Look forward, and make a left middle-level forearm block (*Hidari Uchi Uke*).

Looking forward, draw the right arm up to the right side of the body in an 'L' shape to perform a high-level block (*Migi Jodan Nagashi Uke*), and the left arm to a low-level blocking position (*Hidari Gedan Barai*), then drive the right back fist forwards to high level, supporting the elbow with the back of the left fist (*Migi Jodan Urazuki*). Look to the right and quickly sweep the right foot up to the left thigh (*Migi Nami Ashi*), and drive the supported right arm around to the right of the body to make a middle-level block (*Sokumen Uke*). Look to the left and repeat the same actions – quickly sweep the left foot up to the right thigh (*Hidari Nami Ashi*), and drive around to the left with the right supported arm (*Sokumen Uke*). Look to the right and draw both fists to the left hip (*Koshi Gamae*), and drive both fists to the right side of the body (*Morote Zuki*). Draw the left foot to the right foot and return to *Yoi*.

TEKKI NIDAN

Step to the right with the left foot over the right foot into a crossed-legs stance (*Kosa Dachi*). Draw both fists up the chest to make a middle-level blocking action (*Ryo Hiji Harai Age*). Step to the right with the right foot into a horse-riding stance (*Kiba Dachi*), and drive the raised arms out to the right side of the body (*Sokumen Uke*). Step to the right with the left foot over the right foot into a crossed-legs stance (*Kosa Dachi*) and, at the same time, drive the right arm downwards and forwards to a low-level blocking position supported at the elbow by the left open hand (*Migi Gedan Soete Ude Uke*). Step to the right with the right foot into a horse-riding stance (*Kiba Dachi*) and, using the thumb edge, drive the right fist out to the right side of the body in a low-level blocking position (*Sokumen Soete Gedan*).

Look forward and draw the left foot to the right foot into an informal attention stance (*Heisoku Dachi*), and raise the fists up to the chest (*Ryo Hiji Harai Age*). Look to the left and step with the right foot into a crossed-legs stance (*Kosa Dachi*), then, while stepping to the left into a horse-riding stance (*Kiba Dachi*), drive the raised arms out to the left side of the body (*Sokumen Uke*). Looking to the left, step with the right foot over the left into a crossed-legs stance (*Kosa Dachi*) and, looking forward, drive the left arm downwards and forwards to a low-level blocking position supported by the right open hand (*Gedan Soete Ude Uke*). Looking to the left, step with the left foot into a horse-riding stance (*Kiba Dachi*), then, using the thumb edge, drive the left supported arm out to the left of the body to a low-level blocking position (*Sokumen Soete Gedan*).

Look to the right and draw the fists to the left hip (*Koshi Gamae*), then drive the right supported forearm around to the right to make a middle-level blocking action (*Soete Sokumen Uke*). Look forward and, using the top of the foot, execute a right low-level kick (*Migi Kin Geri*), and step back with the right foot into a horse-riding stance (*Kiba Dachi*); follow this by driving forwards in an outward arc with the right elbow (*Soete Mae Empi*). Look to the right and sweep the right open hand around to the right side of the body (*Sokumen Tate Shuto Uke*), then, drawing the right fist to the right hip, drive across the chest with the left fist (*Hidari Kagi Zuki*).

Step with the left foot over the right foot (*Yoko Sashi Ashi*). Step to the right and drive the outside edge of the right foot to make a rising side kick (*Migi Yoko Geri Keage*), then step into a horse-riding stance (*Kiba Dachi*) and execute a left forearm middle-level block (*Hidari Uchi Uke*). Look forwards, and raise the right arm to the right side of the body in an 'L' shape to a high-level blocking position (*Migi Jodan Nagashi Uke*), and the left arm forwards into a low-level blocking position (*Hidari Gedan Barai*). Then, drive the right fist downwards and forwards to make a high-level back-fist strike, supported at the elbow by the back of the left fist (*Migi Morote Jodan Urazuki*).

Look to the left and draw the fists to the right hip (*Soete Koshi Gamae*). Sweep around with the left supported arm to make a middle-level block (*Soete Sokumen Uke*). Look forwards and, using the top of the left foot, execute a low-level kick (*Hidari Kin Geri*), step back into a horse-riding stance (*Kiba Dachi*), then drive forwards with the left elbow to make a middle-level strike (*Soete Mae Empi*). Sweep around to the left side of the body with the left open hand (*Sokumen Tate Shuto Uke*) and, while drawing the left fist to the left hip, drive across the chest with the right middle-level punch (*Migi Kagi Zuki*).

Step to the left with the right foot over the left foot (*Yoko Sashi Ashi*). Drive out to the left side of the body with the outer edge of the left foot to make a rising kick (*Hidari Yoko Geri Keage*), then step to the left into a horse-riding stance (*Kiba Dachi*). Drive across to the right of the body with the right forearm to make a middle-level block (*Migi Uchi Uke*), then raise the left arm to the left side of the body in an 'L' shape to a high-level blocking position (*Hidari Nagashi Uke*), and the right arm downwards to a low-level blocking position (*Migi Gedan Barai*). Follow this by driving forwards with the left back fist to high level, supported by the back of the right fist under the left elbow (*Hidari Jodan Urazuki*). Draw the left foot to the right foot and return to *Yoi*.

TEKKI SANDAN

Step to the right with the right foot into a horse-riding stance (*Kiba Dachi*). Draw the right fist to the right hip and execute a left middle-level forearm block (*Hidari Chudan Uchi Uke*). Maintain posture, and, while driving the left arm down to a low-level block, execute a right middle-level forearm block (*Kosa Uke*), then draw the forearms together to perform a middle-level trapping block (*Yoko Ude Hasami*). Maintain posture, and drive downwards with the left arm to a low-level blocking position (*Hidari Gedan Barai*), and raise the right arm out to the right of the body in an 'L' shape to a high-level blocking position (*Migi Jodan Nagashi Uke*), then, drawing the back of the left fist to the right elbow, drive downwards and forwards with the back of the right fist to make a back-fist strike (*Migi Jodan Urazuki*). Sliding the arm over the back of the left fist, draw the right fist back until it drops below the left fist, then make a middle-level right-fist strike (*Soete Chudan Zuki*), allowing the left hand to open, and support the right arm at the elbow. Sharply twist the right fist over and make a blocking action (*Soesho Kaeshi Uke*).

Step to the right with left foot over the right foot (*Yoko Sashi Ashi*), then into a horse-riding stance (*Kiba Dachi*). Driving with the thumb edge of the right fist, strike around and downwards to the right side of the body into a low-level blocking position (*Sokumen Gedan Uchi Ude Uke*), then, maintaining the stance, make a large upward winding circle to make a hammer-fist strike to the right of the body (*Migi Sokumen Tettsui Otoshi Uchi*).

Look forwards and drive the right arm under the left fist to make a middle-level punch (*Migi Chudan Zuki*), allowing the left open hand to rest on the right elbow joint. Lower the left arm to a low-level blocking position and raise the right forearm to a middle-level blocking position (*Kosa Uke*), then reverse the position of the arms (*Kosa Uke*), raise the left arm to the left side of the body in an 'L' shape to high level (*Hidari Jodan Urazuki*), then drive the left arm downwards and forwards, supported at the elbow by the back of the right fist (*Hidari Jodan Morote Uraken Uchi*). Look to the left. Step with the right foot over the left foot (*Yoko Sashi Ashi*). Drive to the left with the outside edge of the left foot to make a middle-level rising side kick

(*Hidari Yoko Geri Keage*), then draw both forearms together to make a middle-level trapping block (*Yoko Ude Hasami*). Maintain posture, and draw the left arm out to the left side of the body in an 'L' shape to high level (*Hidari Jodan Nagashi Uke*), then drive the left fist back downwards and forwards to high level (*Hidari Jodan Urazuki*). Draw the left fist back until it drops below the right fist and make a middle-level left-fist strike (*Hidari Chudan Zuki*), allowing the left hand to open, and support the right arm at the elbow.

Step to the left with the right foot over the left (*Yoko Sashi Ashi*). Step with the left foot into a horse-riding stance (*Kiba Dachi*) and, driving with the thumb edge of the left fist, make a low-level strike to the left of the body (*Sokumen Gedan Uchi Ude Uke*), then make a large inward winding circle with the left fist, and make a middle-level hammer-fist strike (*Hidari Sokumen Tettsui Otoshi Uchi*). Look forwards and, drawing the left fist to the left hip, execute a left middle-level punch (*Hidari Chudan Zuki*). Sweep around to the right of the body with the right open hand (*Sokumen Tate Shuto Uke*) and, while drawing the right fist to the right hip, drive the left fist across the chest to make a middle-level punch (*Hidari Kagi Zuki*).

Step to the right with the left foot over the right foot (*Yoko Sashi Ashi*). Drive with the outside edge of the right foot to the right to make a middle-level rising side kick (*Migi Yoko Geri Keage*), then step into a horse-riding stance (*Kiba Dachi*). Execute a left middle-level forearm block (*Hidari Gedan Uchi Uke*), then lower the left arm to a low-level blocking position, and execute a middle-level forearm block with the right arm (*Kosa Uke*). Raise the right arm out to the right side of the body in an 'L' shape at high level (*Migi Jodan Nagashi Uke*), then, raising the back of the left fist to the right elbow, execute a supported middle-level right back-fist strike (*Migi Jodan Soete Urazuki*). Draw the left foot to the right foot and return to *Yoi*.

BASSAI DAI

Step with the right foot, line 6f, into a crossed-legs stance (*Kosa Dachi*) and, drawing the left hand to the inside of the right forearm, execute a middle-level supported block (*Migi Chudan Uchi Ude Uke*). Turn 180 degrees anti-clockwise. Step with the left foot, line 6r, into a front stance (*Zenkutsu Dachi*), and execute a left middle-level forearm block (*Hidari Chudan Uchi Uke*), followed by a right middle-level forearm block (*Migi Chudan Uchi Uke*), and allow the stance to change to half-facing (*Gyaku Hanmi*).

Slide the right foot across and turn the body 180 degrees clockwise, line 6f, and, while executing a left inward winding forearm block (*Hidari Chudan Soto Uke*) change the stance to half-facing (*Gyaku Hanmi*), followed by a right middle-level forearm block (*Migi Chudan Uchi Uke*), allowing the stance to change to front stance (*Zenkutsu Dachi*).

Turn 45 degrees clockwise, line 3, while drawing the feet together, the right foot to the left foot. Bending at the knees, scoop around with the right fist to the right side of the body (*Gedan Sukui Uke*), then, as the right arm is extended to the right of the body, step with right foot, line 3, into a front stance (*Zenkutsu Dachi*). Execute an inward winding middle-level right forearm block (*Migi Chudan Soto Uke*), followed by the same action with the left arm (*Hidari*

Chudan Uchi Uke), changing the stance to half-facing (*Gyaku Hanmi*).

Turn 45 degrees anti-clockwise, line 6f, and stand with the feet slightly apart (*Shizentai*) and draw the fists to the right hip (*Koshi Gamae*). Sweep the left open hand around to the front until it is extended (*Hidari Chudan Tate Shuto Uke*), and execute a right middle-level punch (*Migi Chudan Zuki*). Maintain the foot position and twist the body, so the right side of the body is facing line 6f (*Gyaku Hanmi*), and execute a right middle-level forearm block (*Migi Chudan Uchi Uke*). Return the body to a forward-facing position by turning, and execute a left middle-level punch (*Hidari Chudan Zuki*). Repeat the same action to the right by twisting the body, with the left side of the body facing line 6f (*Gyaku Hanmi*), and execute a left middle-level forearm block (*Hidari Chudan Uchi Uke*).

Step with the right foot, line 6f, into a back stance (*Kokutsu Dachi*), and execute a right middle-level knife-hand block (*Migi Chudan Shuto Uke*). Step with the left foot, line 6f, into a back stance (*Kokutsu Dachi*), and execute a left middle-level knife-hand block (*Hidari Chudan Shuto Uke*). Step with the right foot, line 6f, into a back stance (*Kokutsu Dachi*) and execute a right middle-level knife-hand block (*Migi Chudan Shuto Uke*). Step backwards with the right foot, line 6r, into a back stance (*Kokutsu Dachi*), and execute a left middle-level knife-hand block (*Hidari Chudan Shuto Uke*). Scoop under the left open hand with the right open hand (*Jodan Juji Uke*), and, pulling the hands down towards the lower abdomen, execute a right stamping kick (*Migi Fumikomi*), then, pivoting on the left foot, turn 180 degrees anti-clockwise and step backwards with the right foot, line 6f, into a back stance (*Kokutsu Dachi*), and execute a left middle-level knife-hand block (*Hidari Chudan Shuto Uke*).

Step with the right foot, line 6f, into a back stance (*Kokutsu Dachi*), and execute a middle-level knife-hand block (*Migi Chudan Shuto Uke*). Draw the right foot back to the left foot into an informal attention stance (*Heisoku Dachi*). While raising the right knee up towards the chest, drive both arms upwards to a high-level blocking position (*Morote Age Uke*), then execute a right middle-level front kick (*Migi Mae Geri*), and step forwards with the right foot into a front stance (*Zenkutsu Dachi*), while driving the outside edge of the fists down to make two middle-level hammer-fist strikes (*Chudan Tettsui Hasami Uchi*). Push forwards with the right foot, line 6r, into a front stance (*Zenkutsu Dachi*), and execute a right middle-level punch (*Migi Chudan Oi Zuki*).

Pivoting, turn 180 degrees anti-clockwise, line 6f, change to a front stance (*Zenkutsu Dachi*), and draw the left arm up to the left side of the body in an 'L' shape to a high level and the right open hand down to a low-level blocking position (*Manji Uke*). Draw the left open hand to the right shoulder (*Nagashi Uke*), and drive the right palm heel down to low level (*Migi Gedan Teisho Uchi*). While drawing the left foot to the right foot into an informal attention stance (*Heisoku Dachi*), lower the left fist to a low-level blocking position and raise the right fist up to the right side of the body in an 'L' shape to high level (*Manji Gamae*). Sweep around with the right foot, line 6f, execute a crescent moon kick (*Mikazuki*), lower the right foot into a horse-riding stance (*Kiba Dachi*), then execute a right low-level

block (*Migi Gedan Barai*). Turn the head 180 degrees to face line 6r and sweep the back of the left hand around to the left side of the body (*Hidari Chudan Haishu Uke*).

Pivoting on the left foot, sweep around with the right foot, line 6r, and strike the left open hand by executing a right crescent moon kick (*Mikazuki Geri*). Lower the right foot into a horse-riding stance (*Kiba Dachi*), then strike the left open hand again with the right elbow (*Migi Empi Uchi*). Follow this immediately by driving the right arm down in front of the body to a low-level blocking position (*Migi Gedan Barai*), and bring the left fist to rest on the right upper arm (*Hidari Soete*). Maintain posture, and repeat the same action on the left side (*Hidari Gedan Barai, Migi Soete*). Maintain posture, and repeat the action again on the right side (*Migi Gedan Barai, Hidari Soete*).

Turn to face line 6r and step into a front stance (*Zenkutsu Dachi*) and draw the fists to the left hip (*Koshi Gamae*). Drive the right arm forwards to make a middle-level punch and, at the same time, drive the left fist over the head to make a high-level punch (*Yama Zuki*). Draw the right foot to the left foot into an informal attention stance (*Heisoku Dachi*) and, while turning, bring both fists to rest at the right hip (*Koshi Gamae*). Execute a left front kick along line 6r (*Hidari Mae Geri*), then step with the left foot, line 6r, into a front stance (*Zenkutsu Dachi*). Drive the left arm forwards to make a middle-level punch and, at the same time, drive the right fist over the head to make a high-level punch (*Yama Zuki*).

Draw the left foot to the right foot into an informal attention stance (*Heisoku Dachi*) and, while turning, bring both fists to rest at the left hip (*Koshi Gamae*).

Execute a right front kick along line 6r (*Migi Mae Geri*), then step with the right foot, line 6r, into a front stance (*Zenkutsu Dachi*). Drive the right arm forwards to make a middle-level punch and, at the same time, drive the left fist over the head to make a high-level punch (*Yama Zuki*). Draw the left foot across to line 2 into a front stance (*Zenkutsu Dachi*) and, while drawing the left fist to the left hip, sweep around and downwards with the right fist in a large inward winding circle (*Migi Gedan Sukui Uke*). Pivoting on the balls of the feet, repeat this action on the left side by sweeping around and downwards with the left fist in a large inward winding circle (*Hidari Gedan Sukui Uke*).

Step with the right foot, line 5, into a back stance (*Kokutsu Dachi*), and execute a right middle-level knife-hand block (*Migi Chudan Shuto Uke*). Step backwards with the right foot, line 6r, and draw both arms to the right side of the body with the hands open. Turn to face line 4, and make a skipping action by drawing the right foot to the left foot, then step with the left foot, line 4, into a back stance (*Kokutsu Dachi*), and execute a left knife-hand block (*Hidari Chudan Shuto Uke*). Draw the left foot to the right foot and return to *Yoi*.

KANKU DAI

Standing in the *Yoi* posture, draw both open hands to about 10in (25cm) in front of the lower abdomen. Allow the first two fingers of each hand to cross at the tips – right on left – and the extended thumbs to cross at the tips – right on left. There should be a triangle of space between the thumbs and fingers and all the fingers should be close together, with the palms directed towards the legs. Start to raise the arms forwards and upwards above the head and make a large circle of movement by taking each arm out to either side of the body and back to its original position. At this point, allow the little finger edge of the right hand to press against the palm of the left hand.

Step with the left foot, line 2, into a back stance (*Kokutsu Dachi*). Raise the left arm out to the left side of the body in an 'L' shape (*Hidari Kaishu Haiwan Uke*). Pivot on the heels and turn 180 degrees to line 3 and transfer the weight to the left leg to form a back stance (*Kokutsu Dachi*). Raise the right arm out to the right side of the body in an 'L' shape (*Kaishu Haiwan Uke*). Turn to face line 6f, draw the left foot towards the right foot slightly into a natural posture (*Shizentai*), and sweep the left open hand forward from the right shoulder (*Hidari Chudan Tate Shuto Uke*). Drawing the left hand to the left hip, execute a right middle-level punch (*Migi Chudan Zuki*). Without moving the feet, twist the body to the left, and at the same time draw the right extended arm around to make a middle-level forearm block (*Migi Chudan Uchi Uke*). Turn the body to face forwards, line 6f, and execute a left middle-level punch (*Hidari Chudan Zuki*). Twist the body to the right, and at the same time draw the left extended arm around to make a middle-level forearm block (*Hidari Chudan Uchi Uke*).

Draw the left foot towards the right foot. Turn 45 degrees clockwise, line 3, and draw both fists to the left hip (*Koshi Gamae*). Look towards line 1 and drive upwards and outwards with the outer edge of the right foot to make a right middle-level rising kick (*Migi Chudan Yoko Geri Keage*). At the same time, execute a right high-level back-fist strike (*Migi Jodan*

Uraken Uchi), then, while turning to face line 6f, step backwards with the right foot, line 1, into a back stance (*Kokutsu Dachi*), and execute a left middle-level knife-hand block (*Hidari Chudan Shuto Uke*). Step with the right foot, line 6f, into a back stance (*Kokutsu Dachi*), and execute a right middle-level knife-hand block (*Migi Chudan Shuto Uke*). Step with the left foot, line 6f, into a back stance (*Kokutsu Dachi*), and execute a left middle-level knife-hand block (*Hidari Chudan Shuto Uke*). Step with the right foot, line 6f, into a front stance (*Zenkutsu Dachi*), and execute a right middle-level spear-hand strike (*Migi Chudan Shihon Nukite*).

Pivoting, turn 180 degrees anti-clockwise, line 6r, into a half-facing stance (*Gyaku Hanmi*), execute a right high-level knife-hand block (*Migi Jodan Shuto Uke*), followed immediately by a high-level right-foot kick (*Migi Jodan Mae Geri*), then, pivoting on the left foot, step backwards with the right foot, line 6r, into a back stance (*Kokutsu Dachi*). Raise the right arm out to the right side of the body in an 'L' shape, and the left arm down to a low-level blocking position (*Manji Gamae*). Draw the left fist to the right shoulder (*Hidari Nagashi Uke*), and the right open hand down to a low-level blocking position (*Migi Gedan Shuto Uke*). Draw the right fist to the right hip and lower the left fist down again to a low-level blocking position (*Gedan Gamae*).

While changing to a half-facing stance (*Gyaku Hanmi*), execute a right high-level knife-hand block (*Migi Jodan Shuto Uke*), followed immediately by a high-level right-foot kick (*Migi Jodan Mae Geri*), then, pivoting on the left foot, step backwards with the right foot, line 6f, into a back stance (*Kokutsu Dachi*). Raise the

right arm out to the right side of the body in an 'L' shape, and the left arm down to a low-level blocking position (*Manji Gamae*). Draw the left fist to the right shoulder (*Hidari Nagashi Uke*), and the right open hand down to a low-level blocking position (*Migi Gedan Shuto Uke*). Draw the right fist to the right hip and lower the left fist down again to a low-level blocking position (*Gedan Gamae*).

Turn to face line 8 and draw the fists to the left hip (*Koshi Gamae*), drive upwards and outwards with the outer edge of the left foot to make a middle-level rising kick (*Hidari Chudan Yoko Geri Keage*) and, at the same time, execute a left back-fist strike (*Hidari Jodan Uraken Uchi Uke*), then step along line 8 into a front stance (*Zenkutsu Dachi*). Strike the left open hand with the right elbow (*Migi Mae Empi*).

Turn to face line 7 and draw the fists to the right hip (*Koshi Gamae*), drive upwards and outwards with the outer edge of the right foot to make a middle-level rising kick (*Migi Chudan Yoko Geri Keage*) and, at the same time, execute a right back-fist strike (*Migi Jodan Uraken Uchi Uke*), then step along line 7 into a front stance (*Zenkutsu Dachi*). Strike the right open hand with the left elbow (*Hidari Mae Empi*).

Turn to face line 8 and change the stance to a back stance (*Kokutsu Dachi*), and execute a left middle-level knife-hand block (*Hidari Chudan Shuto Uke*). Step diagonally with the right foot, line 'd', into a back stance (*Kokutsu Dachi*), and execute a right middle-level knife-hand block (*Migi Chudan Shuto Uke*).

Turn to face line 7 and step with the right foot into a back stance (*Kokutsu Dachi*), and execute a right middle-level knife-hand block (*Migi Chudan Shuto*

Uke). Step diagonally with the left foot from line 'c' into a back stance (*Kokutsu Dachi*), and execute a left middle-level knife-hand block (*Hidari Chudan Shuto Uke*).

Step across with the left foot, line 6r, into a half-facing stance (*Gyaku Hanmi*), and execute a right high-level knife-hand block (*Migi Jodan Shuto Uke*), followed immediately by a high-level right-foot kick (*Migi Jodan Mae Geri*). Then, lowering the right foot, draw the left foot to the outside edge of the right foot into a crossed-legs stance (*Kosa Dachi*), and execute a right middle-level forearm block (*Migi Chudan Uraken Uchi*). Step backwards with the left foot, line 6f, into a front stance (*Zenkutsu Dachi*), and execute a right middle-level forearm block (*Migi Chudan Uchi Uke*), followed quickly by a left middle-level reverse punch (*Hidari Chudan Gyaku Zuki*), and a right middle-level punch (*Migi Chudan Zuki*).

Pivoting on the left foot, turn 180 degrees anti-clockwise, line 6f, and at the same time raise the right knee up towards the chest (*Hiza Gamae*), and drive around with the right supported arm to make a middle-level forearm block (*Morote Uke*). Then, with the right foot forwards in a deep stance, lower the body and place the open hands to either side of the right foot with the chest resting almost on the right knee (*Ryote Fuse*). Maintaining the same low position, turn 180 degrees anti-clockwise, line 6r, and execute a left low-level knife-hand block (*Hidari Gedan Shuto Uke*). Rising, step forwards with the right leg, line 6r, into a back stance (*Kokutsu Dachi*), and execute a right middle-level knife-hand block (*Migi Chudan Shuto Uke*).

Turning anti-clockwise, draw the left foot across to line 2 into a back stance (*Kokutsu Dachi*), and execute a left middle-level knife-hand block (*Hidari Chudan Uchi Uke*), then execute a right middle-level reverse punch (*Migi Chudan Gyaku Zuki*). Turning clockwise to line 3, change to a back stance (*Kokutsu Dachi*), and execute a right middle-level knife-hand block (*Migi Chudan Uchi Uke*), then execute a left middle-level reverse punch (*Hidari Chudan Gyaku Zuki*) followed by a right middle-level punch (*Migi Chudan Zuki*).

Draw the left foot towards the right foot and draw the fists to the left hip (*Koshi Gamae*). Look towards line 1, drive upwards and outwards with the outside edge of the right foot to make a middle-level rising kick (*Migi Chudan Yoko Geri Keage*) and, at the same time, execute a right high-level back-fist strike (*Migi Jodan Uraken Uchi*). Then, pivoting on the left foot, turn to face line 6f, and step backwards with the right foot, line 1, into a back stance (*Kokutsu Dachi*), and execute a left middle-level knife-hand block (*Hidari Chudan Shuto Uke*).

Step with the right foot, line 6f, into a front stance (*Zenkutsu Dachi*), and execute a right middle-level spear-hand strike (*Migi Chudan Shihon Nukite*). Twist the extended right open hand anti-clockwise and, rotating the body anti-clockwise, move towards the right hand so that it is positioned behind the body. Then step with the left foot, line 6f, into a horse-riding stance (*Kiba Dachi*), and, drawing the right fist to the right hip, execute a left high-level Hidari back-fist strike (*Hidari Jodan Uraken Uchi*). Make a short sliding movement along line 6f (*Yori Ashi*), and execute a left middle-level hammer-fist strike (*Hidari Chudan Tettsui Uchi*), then strike the left open hand with the right elbow (*Migi Empi Uchi*). Look towards line 6r while remaining in a horse-riding stance (*Kiba Dachi*), and draw both fists to the left hip (*Koshi Gamae*). Execute a right low-level block (*Migi Gedan Barai*).

Turn 180 degrees clockwise, and sweep around with the left foot, line 6r, executing a left crescent moon kick (*Mikazuki*), then stepping into a horse-riding stance, line 6r (*Kiba Dachi*). Drive the left fist down in front of the body to make a left low-level hammer-fist strike (*Ryo Ude Mawashi Uke*), followed by the same action with the right arm (*Migi Otoshi Zuki*). Rise in posture and drive both open hands upwards to high-level blocking positions (*Jodan Shuto Juji Uke*). Maintain the high-level blocking posture, turn clockwise, passing the left foot over the right foot, to face line 6r into a back stance with the right foot forward (*Kokutsu Dachi*) and, at the same time, draw the hands down towards the abdomen (*Juji Gamae*). Leap high and forward, line 6r, and execute a left kick (*Hidari Tobi Geri*), and a right kick (*Migi Tobi Geri*), land in a front stance with the right foot forward (*Zenkutsu Dachi*), and execute a right middle-level forearm block (*Migi Chudan Uraken Uchi*). Turn 180 degrees, draw the left foot to the right foot, to face line 6f, scoop around with the right arm in an inward winding circle (*Sukui Uke*), and return to *Yoi*.

HANGETSU

Step with the left foot, line 6f, into a straddle stance (*Hangetsu Dachi*), and execute a left middle-level forearm block (*Hidari Chudan Uchi Uke*), followed by a right middle-level reverse punch (*Migi Chudan Gyaku Zuki*). Step with the right foot, line 6f, into a straddle stance (*Hangetsu Dachi*),

and execute a right middle-level forearm block (*Migi Chudan Uchi Uke*), followed by a left middle-level reverse punch (*Hidari Chudan Gyaku Zuki*). Step with the left foot, line 6f, into a straddle stance (*Hangetsu Dachi*), and execute a left middle-level forearm block (*Hidari Chudan Uchi Uke*), followed by a right middle-level reverse punch (*Migi Chudan Gyaku Zuki*).

Draw both fists to the nipples with the index knuckle protruding (*Morote Yoko Ken Ate*), and drive both fists forwards until the arms are extended to chest height (*Haito Ippon Ken*). Open both hands and raise them to either side of the body in 'L' shapes (*Kaishu Yama Gamae*), then rotate the arms inwards, passing and crossing at the chest, and out to either side of the body at low-level blocking positions (*Kaishu Ryowan Gamae*).

Turn 180 degrees anti-clockwise to face line 6r, and step back with the right foot, line 6f, into a straddle stance (*Hangetsu Dachi*). At the same time, extend the index finger and thumb of each hand, and fold the second, third and fourth fingers towards the palm of each hand. While in this position, lower the left hand to a low-level blocking position with the palm directed downwards, and raise the right hand up to middle level with the palm directed upwards (*Kaishu Kosa Uke*), then twist the right hand over so the palm is directed downwards (*Migi Kake Dori*).

Repeat this action by stepping forwards with the right foot, line 6r, into a straddle stance (*Hangetsu Dachi*). At the same time, extend the index finger and thumb of each hand, and fold the second, third and fourth fingers towards the palm of each hand. While in this position, lower the right hand to a low-level blocking position with the palm directed downwards, and raise the left hand up to middle level with the palm directed upwards (*Kaishu Kosa Uke*), then twist the left hand over so the palm is directed downwards (*Hidari Kake Dori*).

Repeat this action one more time by stepping forwards with the left foot, line 6r, into a straddle stance (*Hangetsu Dachi*). At the same time, extend the index finger and thumb of each hand, and fold the second, third and fourth fingers towards the palm of each hand. While in this position, lower the left hand to a low-level blocking position with the palm directed downwards, and raise the right hand up to middle level with the palm directed upwards (*Kaishu Kosa Uke*), then twist the right hand over so the palm is directed downwards (*Hidari Kake Dori*).

Step across with the right foot, line 2, into a straddle stance (*Hangetsu Dachi*), and execute a right middle-level forearm block (*Migi Chudan Uchi Uke*), then execute a left middle-level reverse punch (*Hidari Chudan Gyaku Zuki*). Turn 180 degrees anti-clockwise, step across with the left foot, line 3, into a straddle stance (*Hangetsu Dachi*), and execute a left middle-level forearm block (*Hidari Chudan Uchi Uke*), then a right middle-level reverse punch (*Hidari Chudan Gyaku Zuki*). Turn 45 degrees clockwise, and step across with the right foot, line 1, into a straddle stance (*Hangetsu Dachi*), and execute a right middle-level forearm block (*Migi Chudan Uchi Uke*), then execute a left middle-level reverse punch (*Hidari Chudan Gyaku Zuki*).

While turning 180 degrees anti-clockwise, sweep around in an upward and outward winding arc with the left foot, line 6f, and execute a left crescent moon kick (*Hidari Mikazuki*), then step down with the left foot along line 6f into a straddle

stance (*Kokutsu Dachi*), and drive down-wards with the left fist to make a back-fist strike (*Hidari Uraken Zuki*).

Step with the right foot over the left foot (*Hanmi Sashi Ashi*). Drive with the left foot, line 6f, to make a left front kick (*Hidari Mae Geri*), and lower the left foot along line 6f into a straddle stance (*Hangetsu Dachi*). Execute a left low-level block (*Hidari Gedan Barai*), followed by a right middle-level reverse punch (*Migi Chudan Gyaku Zuki*), and a left high-level rising block (*Hidari Jodan Age Uke*).

While turning 180 degrees clockwise, sweep around in an upward and outward winding arc with the right foot, line 6r, and execute a right crescent moon kick (*Migi Mikazuki*), then step down with the right foot along line 6r into a back stance (*Kokutsu Dachi*), and drive downwards with the right fist to make a back-fist strike (*Migi Uraken Zuki*).

Step with the left foot over the right foot (*Hanmi Sashi Ashi*). Drive with the right foot, line 6r, to make a right front kick (*Migi Mae Geri*), and lower the right foot along line 6r into a back stance (*Kokutsu Dachi*). Execute a right low-level block (*Migi Gedan Barai*), followed by a left middle-level reverse punch (*Hidari Chudan Gyaku Zuki*), and a right high-level rising block (*Hidari Jodan Age Uke*).

While turning 180 degrees anti-clockwise, sweep around in an upward and outward winding arc with the left foot, line 6f, and execute a left crescent moon kick (*Hidari Mikazuki*), then step down with the left foot along line 6f into a back stance (*Kokutsu Dachi*), and drive downwards with the left fist to make a back-fist strike (*Migi Uraken Zuki*). Drive around with the right foot and strike the left open hand (*Migi Mikazuki Geri*), step back with the

67

right foot, line 6r, into a front stance (*Zenkutsu Dachi*), and execute a right low-level reverse punch (*Migi Gedan Gyaku Zuki*). Draw the left foot back towards the right foot (*Neko Ashi Dachi*), and drive both open hands – touching at the wrists – into a low-level blocking position (*Teisho Awase Gedan Uke*). Draw the left foot back and return to *Yoi*.

JION

Stand with the feet together, with the right fist at a point 8-9in (20-22cm) in front of the chin, and the palm of the left hand covering the right fist. The elbows are slightly out and the armpits slightly open (*Jiai No Kamae*). Without moving the right foot, step backwards, line 1, with the left foot into a front stance (*Zenkutsu Dachi*). At the same time, perform a left low-level block and a right middle-level block (*Kosa Uke*). The left arm begins the low-level block from the right shoulder, and the right middle-level block starts just at the left elbow.

Step with the left foot diagonally, line 4, into a front stance (*Zenkutsu Dachi*). At the same time, cross the wrists, with the right hand to the inside of the left wrist, and the palms facing towards the body. On completion of the front stance, perform an opening block by extending the right fist in line with the right shoulder and the left fist in line with the left shoulder. As the fists reach shoulder height, turn them so the palms are facing outwards away from the body (*Kakiwake Uke*). The intention of the movement is to push your arms between the arms of an attacker who is trying to grasp your clothing around the neck.

Having exposed the body of the attacker, make a right middle-level kick to the solar plexus (*Migi Chudan Mae Geri*), and allow the foot to land firmly into a front stance (*Zenkutsu Dachi*), line 4. The kick should be made immediately after the opening block in the previous move, and should be sufficient to cause the opponent to double up rather than driving him away.

As you land in a front stance, the attacker should still be close enough to strike. Make three rapid middle-level fist strikes to the attacker's upper body, one with the right fist (*Migi Chudan Zuki*), followed with the left fist (*Hidari Gyaku Zuki*), then once again with the right fist (*Migi Chudan Zuki*). These three strikes should be performed quickly but smoothly, with the second and third strikes being slightly faster than the first.

Step with the right foot diagonally, line 5, into a front stance (*Zenkutsu Dachi*). At the same time, cross the wrists, with the right hand to the inside of the left wrist, and the palms facing towards the body. On completion of the front stance, perform an opening block by extending the right fist in line with the right shoulder and the left fist in line with the left shoulder. As the fists reach shoulder height, turn them so the palms are facing outwards away from the body (*Kakiwake Uke*).

Having exposed the body of the attacker, make a left middle-level kick (*Hidari Chudan Mae Geri*) to the solar plexus, and allow the foot to land firmly into a front stance (*Zenkutsu Dachi*), line 5. The kick should be made immediately after the opening block in the previous move, and should be sufficient to cause the opponent to double up rather than driving him away.

As you land in a front stance, the attacker should still be close enough to strike. Make three rapid middle-level fist strikes to the attacker's upper body, one with the right fist (*Migi Chudan Zuki*), followed with the left fist (*Hidari Gyaku Zuki*), then once again with the right fist (*Migi Chudan Zuki*). These three strikes should be performed quickly but smoothly, with the second and third strikes being slightly faster than the first.

Transfer the weight to the right leg and step forwards on the left foot into a front stance (*Zenkutsu Dachi*), line 6f. At the same time as this step is made, raise the right arm into a high-level covering action. This block is like a high-level block but with an open hand, with the palm facing away from the body. Draw the right fist back to the hip and raise the left arm to a high-level block (*Migi Jodan Age Uke*). While maintaining a firm front stance, draw the left fist to the left hip and execute a middle-level right-fist strike (*Migi Chudan Gyaku Zuki*). The two high-level blocks in the previous section and the strike in this section should be carried out smoothly and fairly quickly.

Step forwards with the right foot into a front stance (*Zenkutsu Dachi*), line 6f. Perform a left high-level covering block with the left hand open and the palm facing away from the body, then, retracting the left fist to the left hip, perform a right high-level block (*Migi Jodan Age Uke*). The stepping into front stance and the two blocks should finish at the same time. Maintain the stance, and execute a middle-level fist strike (*Hidari Chudan Gyaku Zuki*). Step forwards with the left foot into a front stance, line 6f. At the same time as this step is made, raise the right arm into a high-level covering block (*Migi Jodan Haishu Age Uke*), then draw the right fist back to the hip and raise the left arm to a high-level block (*Hidari Jodan Age Uke*). Step forwards with the right foot (*Zenkutsu Dachi*), line 6f, and at the same time execute a middle-level right-fist strike (*Migi Chudan Zuki*).

Using the left foot, make a three-quarter turn anti-clockwise and step into a back stance (*Kokutsu Dachi*), line 12. While turning, allow the arms to cross by the solar plexus parallel to each other, then raise the right arm up to the right side of the body in a high-level block, and the left arm into a left low-level block (*Manji Uke*). The right arm is angled to 45 degrees, with the palm of the fist facing to the left, and the attention is focused on the left low-level block. The whole action should be completed when the back stance is confirmed. The intention here is to block a strike to the lower body with the left arm, and a strike to the head with the right arm.

Take the weight off the left foot and, pushing with the right foot, make a quick shuffling movement (*Yori Ashi*), and change to a horse-riding stance. At the same time, bring the left fist to the left hip, and the right arm across the solar plexus (*Migi Chudan Kagi Zuki*). The right fist should be level with the left side of the chest, and the arm angled down slightly. There should be a 5 to 6-in gap between the arm and the chest.

Turn to look to the right and step into a back stance (*Kokutsu Dachi*), line 11. Allow the arms to cross by the solar plexus parallel to each other, then raise the left arm up to the left side of the body in a high-level block, and the right arm into a right low-level block (*Manji Uke*). The left arm is angled to 45 degrees, with the palm of the fist facing to the right, and the attention is focused on the right low-level block.

Take the weight off the right foot and, pushing with the left foot, make a quick shuffling movement (*Yori Ashi*), and change to a horse-riding stance (*Kiba Dachi*). At the same time bring the right fist to the right hip, and the left arm across the solar plexus (*Hidari Chudan Kagi Zuki*). The left fist should be level with the right side of the chest, and the arm angled down slightly. There should be a 5 to 6-in gap between the arm and the chest.

Step with the left foot, line 6r, into a front stance (*Zenkutsu Dachi*). At the same time, bring the right fist to the right hip, and with the left arm perform a low-level block (*Hidari Gedan Barai*).

Slide forwards with the right foot into a horse-riding stance (*Kiba Dachi*). With the attention directed towards the starting point, drive the right fist out to the right side of the body, allowing the hand to open, and perform a palm heel thrust (*Migi Teishu Uchi*). Draw the left fist to the left hip.

Repeat the previous movement to the opposite side – slide forwards with the left foot into a horse-riding stance (*Kiba Dachi*). With the attention directed towards the starting point, drive the left fist out to the left side of the body, allowing the hand to open, and perform a palm heel thrust (*Hidari Teishu Uchi*). Draw the right fist to the right hip.

Repeat this action one more time by sliding forwards with the right foot into a horse-riding stance (*Kiba Dachi*). With the attention directed towards the starting point, drive the right fist out to the right side of the body, allowing the hand to open, and perform a palm heel thrust (*Migi Teishu Uchi*). Draw the left fist to the left hip. At the end of this sequence of moves you should have returned close to the starting point.

Turn the body 45 degrees anti-clockwise and step into a back stance with the left foot forward and the weight on the right leg (*Kokutsu Dachi*), line 2. While turning, allow the arms to cross by the solar plexus parallel to each other, then raise the right arm up to the right side of the body in a high-level block, and the left arm into a left low-level block (*Manji Uke*). The right arm is angled to 45 degrees, with the palm of the fist facing to the left, and the attention is focused on the left low-level block.

Draw the right foot to the left foot into an attention stance (*Heisoku Dachi*), and perform a high-level block (*Jodan Morote Uke*). The left arm should be angled at 45 degrees with the fist level with the head and the palm facing inwards. The right fist is pushed under the left elbow in a supporting action, with the right elbow covering the solar plexus.

The last two sequences are repeated in the opposite direction – turn to the right, and step out into a back stance (*Kokutsu Dachi*), line 3. While turning, allow the arms to cross by the solar plexus parallel to each other, then raise the left arm up to the left side of the body in a high-level block, and the right arm into a right low-level block (*Manji Uke*). The left arm is angled to 45 degrees, with the palm of the fist facing inwards, and the attention is focused on the right low-level block.

Continue the sequence by drawing the left foot to the right foot into an attention stance (*Heisoku Dachi*), and perform a high-level block (*Jodan Morote Uke*). The right arm should be angled at 45 degrees, with the fist level with the head and the palm facing inwards. The left fist is pushed under the right elbow in a supporting action, with the left elbow covering the solar plexus.

Maintain the attention stance (*Heisoku*

Dachi). Rotate both arms in complete circles past the face and body, the left arm in a clockwise direction, and the right arm in an anti-clockwise direction. The arms should cross by the face and drive downwards and outwards until they are level with the hips on either side. The hands are open with the palms facing towards the hips and there should be about 12in (30cm) of space between each palm and the hips (*Ryowan Gamae*).

Draw the fists back to the hips and step forwards with the right foot (*Kosa Dachi*), line 6f, and drive both fists downwards and forwards, allowing them to cross at the wrists (*Gedan Juji Uke*). The wrists should be positioned about 9 or 10in (25cm) from the right knee with the fingers facing downwards. The body must remain upright. Draw backwards with the left foot into a front stance (*Zenkutsu Dachi*), line 6r. Drive both arms out to either side of the body until they are in line with, and about 18in (45cm) away from, the hips. The fists should be closed with the palms facing downwards (*Ryowan Gedan Kakiwake*).

Step forwards with the left foot into a front stance (*Zenkutsu Dachi*), line 6f. Raise the right fist to the left shoulder with the back of the fist to the face and the elbow close to the chest. Drive forwards in a diagonal line from left to right until the fist is level with the right shoulder and in line with the right knee. The arm should be bent at the elbow in a 'V' shape. When this point is reached, allow the fist to turn clockwise until the palm is facing upwards. Raise the left fist to the right shoulder with the back of the fist to the face and the elbow close to the chest. Drive forwards in a diagonal line from right to left until the fist is level with the left shoulder and in line with the right fist. The arm should be

bent at the elbow in a 'V' shape. When this point is reached, allow the fist to turn clockwise until the palm is facing upwards (*Sowan Uchi Uke*). These two actions are carried out at the same time, allowing the arms to cross at the chest towards the beginning of the movements.

Step forwards with the right foot into a front stance (*Zenkutsu Dachi*), drive both fists upwards and forwards, allowing them to cross at the wrists. The wrists should be positioned at about eye level with the palms facing away from the body (*Jodan Juji Uke*).

Maintain the stance. Draw the left arm back towards the head in a high-level block (*Age Uke*). At the same time, draw the right arm back to the right shoulder then drive it forwards to make a high-level strike (*Migi Urazuki*).

Maintain the stance. Push the left arm forward to a middle-level position (*Chudan*). Raise the right arm until the upper arm is parallel with the right shoulder, and the forearm is directed upwards in a vertical line. The fist is closed and the fingers directed away from the right side of the head (*Migi Jodan Nagashi Uke*).

Maintain the stance. Drive forwards with the right fist to make a high-level strike. The palm of the fist should be directed upwards and the arm should be bent at the elbow in a 'V' shape (*Migi Jodan Urazuki*). At the same time as the strike is made, bring the left fist to rest under the right elbow with the palm facing downwards.

Make a three-quarter anti-clockwise turn, line 12. Step with the left foot into a front stance (*Zenkutsu Dachi*). Raise the left fist to the right shoulder with the back of the fist to the face and the elbow close to the chest. Drive forwards in a diagonal line from right to left until the fist is level with the left shoulder and in line with the left knee. The arm should be bent at the elbow in a 'V' shape. When this point is reached, allow the fist to turn anti-clockwise until the palm is facing upwards (*Hidari Chudan Uchi Uke*). While performing this action, draw the right fist back to the right hip with the fingers facing upwards.

Step with the right foot into a front stance, line 12, and drive forwards with the right fist to make a middle-level strike (*Migi Chudan Oi Zuki*).

Turn 180 degrees while stepping backwards with the right foot into a front stance, line 11. Raise the right fist to the left shoulder with the back of the fist to the face and the elbow close to the chest. Drive forwards in a diagonal line from left to right until the fist is level with the right shoulder and in line with the right knee. The arm should be bent at the elbow in a 'V' shape. When this point is reached, allow the fist to turn clockwise until the palm is facing upwards (*Migi Chudan Uchi Uke*). While performing this action, draw the left fist back to the left hip with the fingers facing upwards. Step with the left foot into a front stance, line 11, and drive forwards with the left fist to make a middle-level strike (*Hidari Chudan Oi Zuki*).

Make a 45-degree turn while stepping with the left foot into a front stance, line 6r (*Zenkutsu Dachi*). Raise the left fist to the right shoulder, palm to the side of the face. Drive the back of the fist down to a point about 6in (15cm) above the left knee. When this point is reached, allow the fist to turn anti-clockwise so the palm is facing the left knee (*Gedan Barai*). While performing this action, draw the right fist back to the

right hip with the fingers facing upwards.

Step with the right foot, line 6r, and perform a low-level stamping kick (*Fumikomi*) and step down into a horse-riding stance (*Kiba Dachi*). At the same time, raise the right arm above the head and, as the low-level kick (*Fumikomi*) is made, drive the right arm downwards in front of the body until it is in line with the abdomen. The fingers should be facing towards the body and the little finger edge of the left hand directed towards the floor (*Migi Otoshi Uke*).

Step with the left foot, line 6r and repeat the above actions – perform a low-level stamping kick (*Fumikomi*) and step into a horse-riding stance (*Kiba Dachi*). At the same time, raise the left arm above the head and, as the low-level kick (*Fumikomi*) is made, drive the left arm downwards in front of the body until it is in line with the abdomen. The fingers should be facing towards the body and the little finger edge of the left hand directed towards the floor (*Migi Otoshi Uke*).

Step with the right foot, line 6r, and repeat the above actions again – perform a low-level stamping kick (*Fumikomi*) and step into a horse-riding stance (*Kiba Dachi*). At the same time, raise the right arm above the head and, as the low-level kick (*Fumikomi*) is made, drive the right arm downwards in front of the body until it is in line with the abdomen. The fingers should be facing towards the body and the little finger edge of the left hand directed towards the floor (*Migi Otoshi Uke*).

Step across with the left foot anti-clockwise into a low attention stance (*Heisoku Dachi*), line 2, and at the same time reach across with the right open hand to the left side of the body. The palm should be facing downwards and the fingers pressed together (*Jodan Tsukami Uke*). Step with the left foot, line 2, into a horse-riding stance (*Kiba Dachi*). Draw the left fist across the chest until it is level with the right side of the chest, with the fingers directed downwards and the fist about 6in (15cm) away from the chest. Draw the right fist back to a point level with the right shoulder, with the fingers directed downwards and the thumb edge of the hand about 6in (15cm) away from the right shoulder. At the same time, drive the left fist in a semi-circle away from the body and out to the side until it is level with the left side of the body. All the movements described here, from the point of the low attention stance (*Heisoku Dachi*), should be performed as one action (*Hidari Yumi Zuki*).

Turn the head 180 degrees to face line 3. Reach across with the left open hand to the right side of the body. The palm should be facing downwards and the fingers pressed together (*Jodan Tsukami Uke*). Pushing with the left foot, make a short sliding movement to the right (*Yori Ashi*). Draw the right fist across the chest until it is level with the left side of the chest, with the fingers directed downwards and the fist about 6in (15cm) away from the chest. Draw the left fist back to a point level with the left shoulder, with the fingers directed downwards and the thumb edge of the hand about 6in (15cm) away from the left shoulder. At the same time, drive the right fist in a semi-circle away from the body and out to the side until it is level with the right side of the body (*Hidari Yumi Zuki*). All the movements described here, from the point of the low attention stance (*Heisoku Dachi*), should be performed as one action.

Draw the right foot to the left foot and turn to face line 6f. Stand with feet together (*Heisoku Dachi*). The right fist should be drawn to a point 8 to 9in (20-22cm) in front of the chin, and the palm of the left hand covering the right fist. The elbows are slightly out and the armpits slightly open (*Jiai No Kamae*).

EMPI

Look forward, line 6f, but turn the body to face left and step out with the left foot, line 2. Go down on one knee by bending the right leg until the knee touches the floor. The sole of the right foot is facing to the right, and the right knee is in line with the left foot. This is rather like turning into a front stance, but going down on one knee instead of remaining standing (*Tachi Hiza*). While sinking down into *Tachi Hiza*, execute a right low-level block (*Migi Gedan Barai*). At the end of the block, the right arm and fist should be in line with the right leg, with the palm facing the right thigh. At the same time, allow the left fist to slide up the right arm to a position at the upper arm between the elbow and the shoulder. The aim here is to block a low-level kick and grab the attacker's ankle or clothing.

Rise up into a horse-riding stance (*Kiba Dachi*), facing line 6f, and draw the left fist to the left hip, with the palm facing upwards, and bring the right fist to rest on the left fist with the palm facing the body and the little finger edge of the hand resting on the left fist fingers (*Koshi Gamae*). The intention here is that, having grabbed the ankle or clothing of the attacker in the previous movement, the rising action of the body and the twisting of the hand causes the attacker to fall over.

Step to the right in front stance (*Zenkutsu Dachi*), line 3, and execute a right low-level block (*Migi Gedan Barai*). Follow this by resuming the horse-riding stance (*Kiba Dachi*), facing line 6f, drawing the right fist to the right hip, and the left arm across the chest (*Hidari Kagi Zuki*). The fist of the left arm should be level with the right side of the ribs, and the arm should be very slightly sloping downwards. There should be a 4 to 5-in gap between the arm and the chest. The arms should reach this position at the same time as the horse-riding stance is assumed.

Step forwards into a front stance, line 6f, and execute a left low-level block (*Hidari Gedan Barai*). While drawing the left fist to the left hip, make a forward right high-level strike (*Migi Jodan Age Zuki*). The line of this strike is arched from the hip to high level. The intention here is to strike the opponent under the chin. At the end of the strike leave the fist at high-level position and open the hand. The fingers should be facing forward and the palm directed towards the floor.

Perform a high-level right front kick (*Migi Jodan Mae Geri*) to the point where the right hand is positioned, step forwards, line 6f, on to the right foot and draw the left foot to a position just behind the right foot (*Kosa Dachi*). The legs should be crossed at the calves and the left ball of the foot should be touching the floor next to the outer edge of the right foot. At the same time as the forward step is made, close the fingers of the right hand to form a fist (*Kami Zukami*). Draw the right fist to the left shoulder (*Migi Nagashi Uke*) and execute a middle-level strike with the left fist (*Hidari Chudan Zuki*), aiming just below the right arm.

Without moving the right foot, step backwards with the left foot, line 6r and, at the same time, while still looking forwards

but with the body turned to line 6r, perform a low-level block (*Ushiro Gedan Barai*) and draw the left fist to the left hip. The position of the stance here is that of performing a low-level block to the rear. In other words, the body has turned to face the starting point of the *Kata*, the attention is focused to the front, and the block is over the right leg. The intention here is that, having made a strike to the attacker's chin, the attacker has grasped hold of the right arm or sleeve. By drawing the right arm back while stepping forwards with the left foot, the grasp is broken, a strike is made to the abdomen, and a low-level block is made to the attacker's right arm.

Turn the head 180 degrees anti-clockwise. Step forwards into a front stance, line 6r, and execute a left low-level block (*Hidari Gedan Barai*). While drawing the left fist to the left hip, make a forward right high-level strike (*Migi Jodan Age Zuki*). The line of this strike is arched from the hip to high level. The intention here is to strike the opponent under the chin. At the end of the strike, leave the fist at high-level position and open the hand. The fingers should be facing forward and the palm should be directed towards the floor.

Perform a high-level right front kick (*Migi Jodan Mae Geri*) to the point where the right hand is positioned, step forwards, line 6r, on to the right foot and draw the left foot to a position just behind the right foot (*Kosa Dachi*). The legs should be crossed at the calves and the left ball of the foot should be touching the floor next to the outer edge of the right foot. At the same time as the forward step is made, close the fingers of the right hand to form a fist. Draw the right fist to the left shoulder (*Migi Nagashi Uke*) and execute a middle-level strike with the left fist (*Hidari*

Chudan Zuki), aiming just below the right arm.

Without moving the right foot, step backwards, line 6f, with the left foot and, at the same time, while still looking forwards but with the body turned to line 6f, perform a low-level block (*Ushiro Gedan Barai*) and draw the left fist to the left hip. The position of the stance here is that of performing a low-level block to the rear. In other words, the body has turned to face away from the starting point of the *Kata*, the attention is focused to the rear, and the block is over the right leg. The intention here is that, the defender having made a strike to the attacker's chin, the attacker has grasped hold of the defender's right arm or sleeve. The defender draws the right arm back while stepping forwards with the left foot, and the grasp is broken, a strike is made to the abdomen, and a low-level block is made to the attacker's right arm.

Turn to face line 6f, change to a front stance (*Zenkutsu Dachi*), and execute a left low-level block (*Hidari Gedan Barai*). Looking forwards, line 6f, draw the left leg and left arm towards and in front of the right leg in an anti-clockwise direction. Continue the sweeping movement with the left leg and lower it into a horse-riding stance (*Kiba Dachi*), line 2. The left arm, having moved in rhythm with the left leg, performs a high-level open-hand block (*Jodan Haishu Uke*). The open hand should be at eye level. The thumb edge of the left arm should be facing the left side of the body, and the left hand should be level with the left eye, palm towards the face.

Draw the right foot up and behind the left knee so that the top of the foot is touching the back of the left leg (*Kataashi Dachi*). At the same time, draw the right

fist across the lower torso in a clockwise direction and continue the movement upwards along the inside of the left arm, which is still in its blocking position, until it is level with the right shoulder, then execute an elbow strike by driving the right forearm on to the left open hand (*Empi Uchi*). The right arm and left hand should be vertically aligned. The intention here is to release a grasp made to the right arm by pulling the opponent to the front and trapping the arm between your own arms. At this point, make a spiritual shout (*Kiai*).

Lower the right foot to resume the horse-riding stance (*Kiba Dachi*), line 3. At the same time, cross the arms so the right arm is facing left with the fist closed, and the left arm is facing right with the hand open. At this point, both arms are parallel. While drawing the right fist back to the right hip, sweep the left open hand around and out to a point directly in front of the body, line 6f, at chest height (*Hidari Chudan Tate Shuto Uke*). The intention here is to block an oncoming strike to the chest or sternum. Follow this with a right then left middle-level fist strike (*Migi Chudan Zuki, Hidari Chudan Zuki*).

Turn and step to the left, line 2, into front stance (*Zenkutsu Dachi*) and execute a left low-level block (*Hidari Gedan Barai*) followed by a right high-level fist strike (*Migi Jodan Age Zuki*). The line of this strike is arched from the hip to high level. The intention here is to strike the opponent under the chin. Step forwards with the right foot, line 2, into a back stance (*Kokutsu Dachi*) and execute a right knife-hand block (*Migi Chudan Shuto Uke*).

Draw the right foot back to the left, then step forward, line 2, with the left foot into another back stance (*Kokutsu Dachi*) and execute a left knife-hand strike (*Hidari*

Chudan Shuto Uke) followed immediately by a right middle-level fist strike (*Migi Chudan Gyaku Zuki*). Step forwards, line 2, with the right foot into another back stance (*Kokutsu Dachi*) and execute a right hand knife block (*Migi Chudan Shuto Uke*).

Turn 180 degrees anti-clockwise into a front stance, line 3 (*Zenkutsu Dachi*), and execute a left low-level block. While drawing the left fist to the left hip, make a forward right high-level strike (*Migi Jodan Age Zuki*). The line of this strike is arched from the hip to high level. The intention here is to strike the opponent under the chin. At the end of the strike leave the fist at high-level position and open the hand. The fingers should be facing forwards and the palm should be directed towards the floor.

Perform a high-level right front kick (*Migi Jodan Mae Geri*) to the point where the right hand is positioned, step forwards, line 3, on to the right foot and draw the left foot to a position just behind the right foot (*Kosa Dachi*). The legs should be crossed at the calves and the left ball of the foot should be touching the floor next to the outer edge of the right foot. At the same time as the forward step is made, close the fingers of the right hand to form a fist. Draw the right fist to the left shoulder (*Migi Nagashi Uke*), and execute a middle-level strike with the left fist (*Hidari Chudan Zuki*), aiming just below the right arm.

Without moving the right foot, step backwards with the left foot and, at the same time, while still looking forward but with the body turned to line 3, perform a low-level block (*Ushiro Gedan Barai*) and draw the left fist to the left hip. The position of the stance here is that of perform-

ing a low-level block to the rear. In other words, the body has turned to face the starting point of the *Kata*, the attention is focused to the front, and the block is over the right leg. The intention here is that, the defender having made a strike to the attacker's chin, the attacker has grasped hold of the defender's right arm or sleeve. The defender draws the right arm back while stepping forwards with the left foot, the grasp is broken, a strike is made to the abdomen, and a low-level block is made to the attacker's right arm.

Turn to the left, line 2, into a front stance (*Zenkutsu Dachi*), and execute a left low-level block (*Hidari Gedan Barai*). Maintain the front stance but turn the head to face line 6f. Draw the left fist to the left hip and raise the right palm heel to the front and centre (*Migi Teishu Uke*). The right hand should be bent at the wrist with the palm facing upwards and with the fingertips pointing downward, and the arm, bent at the elbow, positioned to a 'V' shape. The armpit should be closed and the elbow about 3in (8cm) away from the left side of the ribs.

Move the weight to the left foot and step forwards with the right foot into a front stance (*Zenkutsu Dachi*). At the same time, raise the left hand with the palm facing upwards and lower the right with the palm facing downwards, then change the hands to a reverse order – the right palm facing upwards and the left palm facing downwards (*Teishu Kosa Uke*). These two blocking movements are performed fairly quickly so that the right-hand block with the palm facing upwards is finished in time with the stepping of the right foot into front stance. To achieve this timing, make the first two arm movements when the weight is transferred to the left leg and the next two when the right foot is put forwards into front stance.

Step forwards with the left foot, line 6f (*Zenkutsu Dachi*), and at the same time reverse the blocks (*Teishu Kosa Uke*) – the right hand palm facing downwards and the left hand palm facing upwards. Follow this quickly by stepping through with the right foot, line 6f (*Zenkutsu Dachi*) and once again changing the direction of the blocks (*Teishu Kosa Uke*) – the right hand palm facing upwards and the left hand palm facing downwards. At this point, without moving the feet, change to a back stance and execute a low-level block.

Change to a front stance, line 6f, and at the same time thrust the hands forwards (*Morote Koko Gamae*). The hands are open, with the right arm position as it would be in a high-level block, palm facing forwards and the little finger edge pointing upwards. The intention with this action is to grasp the throat of the attacker, pushing the fingers into the left side of the windpipe and the thumb into the right side of the windpipe. The right hand is thrust forwards in vertical alignment with the left, with the palm facing forwards and the thumb edge of the hand directed away from the right side of the body. The intention might also be that of grasping a vertical bo staff towards the top and bottom. In the first intention the attacker is thrown to one side, and in the second intention the bo staff is twisted, forcing the attacker's arms to cross against each other and sending him off balance. In both intentions the movements remain the same.

Follow this action immediately by turning the body in a half-circle, transferring the weight to the left leg and leaping high into the air (*Joho Kaiten Tobi*), while turning full circle, and landing in a back stance (*Kokutsu Dachi*) with the right foot forward and the weight on the back leg. The intention here is either to jump over the body of the attacker just dealt with, or to escape an attack to the legs by a bo staff or sword. Execute a right knife-hand block (*Migi Chudan Shuto Uke*) at the point of landing.

Step backwards into another back stance (*Kokutsu Dachi*) with the left foot forward and the weight on the right leg. Execute a left knife-hand block (*Hidari Chudan Shuto Uke*).

JUTTE

From the *Jutte Yoi* posture (*Jiai No Kamae*), step backwards with the left foot, line 1, into a front stance (*Zenkutsu Dachi*). Rotate the right open hand from under the left palm and press the back of the right hand downwards to a middle-level blocking position (*Migi Tekubi Kake Uke*). Step with the left foot, line 4, into a front stance (*Zenkutsu Dachi*). Drive the left palm heel downwards to low level, and the right palm heel upwards to middle level (*Teishu Morote Uke*). Look to line 3, and drive the left palm heel out to the right side of the body past the right shoulder (*Hidari Haito Uke*). Step with the right foot, line 3, into a horse-riding stance (*Kiba Dachi*), and drive the thumb edge of the right hand out to the right side of the body to middle level (*Migi Haito Uke*).

Sweep around with the right foot, line 6f, into a horse-riding stance (*Kiba Dachi*), and drive the right palm heel out to the right side of the body at middle level (*Migi Teishu Uke*). Sweep around with the left foot, line 6f, into a horse-riding stance (*Kiba Dachi*), and drive the left palm heel out to the left side of the body at middle level (*Hidari Teishu Uke*). Sweep around with the right foot, line 6f, into a horse-riding stance (*Kiba Dachi*), and drive the right palm heel out to the right side of the body at middle level (*Migi Teishu Uke*).

Look to line 11. Step with the right foot over the left foot, line 6r, into a crossed-legs stance (*Kosa Dachi*), and at the same time raise both arms to high-level blocking positions (*Jodan Juji Uke*). Step with the left foot, line 6r, into a horse-riding stance (*Kiba Dachi*), and lower the arms out to either side of the body to low-level blocking positions (*Ryowan Gedan Kakiwake*). Step with the right foot over the left foot, line 6r, into a crossed-legs stance (*Kosa Dachi*), then step with the left foot, line 6r, into a horse-riding stance (*Kiba Dachi*), and raise both arms out to either side of the body in 'L' shapes (*Yama Kakiwake*).

Maintain the raised arm posture, and sweep around with the left foot, line 6f, to make a left crescent moon kick (*Mikazuki*), and step down with the left foot into a horse-riding stance (*Kiba Dachi*) and, at the same time as the step is made, rotate the left fist clockwise and back again (*Yama Kakiwake*). Maintain the raised arm posture, and sweep around with the right foot, line 6f, to make a right crescent moon kick (*Mikazuki*), and step down with the right foot into a horse-riding stance (*Kiba Dachi*) and, at the same time as the step is made, rotate the right fist anti-clockwise and back again (*Yama Kakiwake*). Maintain the raised arm posture, and sweep around with the left foot, line 6f, to make a left crescent moon kick (*Mikazuki*), and step down with the left foot into a horse-riding stance (*Kiba Dachi*) and, at the same time as the step is made, rotate the left fist clockwise and back again (*Yama Kakiwake*).

Look to line 12, draw the left foot slightly to the right foot into a natural posture (*Shizentai*), and lower the arms out to either side of the body to low-level blocking position (*Ryowan Gamae*). Look to line 6r, step with the right foot into a front stance (*Zenkutsu Dachi*), and drive the right open hand upwards to high level (*Migi Jodan Shuto Uke*), then drive the left hand forwards to a low-level blocking position (*Morote Jo Uke*). Rotate the hands 180 degrees (*Morote Koko Dori*) and, at the same time, draw the left foot around to the right knee so the left side of the body is directed along line 6r (*Sagi Ashi Dachi*), and draw the hands back to the right side of the body – the left arm level with the abdomen and the right arm level with the head (*Morote Jo Dori*). Step with the left foot, line 6r, into a front stance (*Zenkutsu Dachi*), and drive both hands forwards, the left at low level and the right at high level (*Morote Jo Tsuki Dashi*). Rotate the hands 180 degrees (*Morote Koko Dori*) and, at the same time, draw the right foot around to the left knee so the right side of the body is directed along line 6r (*Sagi Ashi Dachi*); draw the hands back to the left side of the body – the right arm level with the abdomen and the left arm level with the head (*Morote Jo Dori*). Step with the right foot, line 6r, into a front stance (*Zenkutsu Dachi*), and drive both hands forwards, the right at low level and the left at high level (*Morote Jo Tsuki Dashi*).

Turn anti-clockwise to face line 2 and step with the left foot into a back stance (*Kokutsu Dachi*) and, at the same time, raise the right arm out to the right side of the body in an 'L' shape, and lower the left arm to a low-level blocking position (*Manji Gamae*). Repeat this action by turning clockwise to face line 3 and, pivoting on the heels, assume a back stance (*Kokutsu Dachi*); at the same time, raise the left arm out to the left side of the body in an 'L' shape, and lower the right arm to a low-level blocking position (*Manji Gamae*).

Draw the left foot to the right foot into an informal attention stance (*Heisoku Dachi*) and, at the same time, raise the right open hand to high level to perform a covering block, then step with the left foot, line 6f, into a front stance (*Zenkutsu Dachi*), and execute a left high-level rising block (*Hidari Jodan Uke*), followed by stepping with the right foot, line 6f, into a front stance (*Zenkutsu Dachi*), and executing a right high-level rising block (*Migi Age Uke*).

Maintaining the right arm posture, step across with the left foot and turn 180 degrees anti-clockwise, line 6r, into a front stance (*Zenkutsu Dachi*), using the right raised open hand as a covering block. Then, drawing the right hand down to the right hip, drive upwards with the left arm to perform a high-level rising block (*Hidari Jodan Age Uke*). Step with the right foot, line 6r, into a front stance (*Zenkutsu Dachi*), and execute a right high-level rising block (*Migi Age Uke*). Turn 180 degrees anti-clockwise and return to *Yoi*.

GANKAKU

Step backwards with the right foot, line 1, into a back stance (*Kokutsu Dachi*). Drive both open hands to high level (*Haishu Awase Uke*) and, drawing the hand back to the right hip, execute a left middle-level hammer-fist strike (*Hidari Chudan Tettsui Zuki*), followed by a right reverse middle-level punch (*Migi Chudan Gyaku Zuki*). Turn 180 degrees anti-clockwise, line 1, execute a right foot crescent moon kick

(*Migi Mikazuki*), and step into a horse-riding stance (*Kiba Dachi*), then execute a right low-level block (*Migi Gedan Barai*).

Turn anti-clockwise, line 6f, into a front stance (*Zenkutsu Dachi*). Allowing the open hands to cross at the wrist, drive them upwards to a high-level blocking position (*Jodan Kaishu Juji Uke*). Follow this by leaping into the air and making two kicks (*Mae Tobi Geri*), landing with the left foot forwards in a front stance (*Zenkutsu Dachi*), then driving downwards with both fists allowing them to cross at the wrist (*Gedan Juji Uke*).

Turn clockwise 180 degrees, line 6r, and step with the left foot, line 6r, into a front stance (*Zenkutsu Dachi*), then drive downwards with both fists allowing them to cross at the wrist (*Gedan Juji Uke*).

Turn clockwise 180 degrees, line 6f, transfer the body weight to the left leg, changing to a back stance (*Kokutsu Dachi*), and drive both open hands down to a low-level blocking position (*Juji Uke*). Step with the left foot, line 6f, into a back stance (*Kokutsu Dachi*), and drive both open hands down to a low-level blocking position (*Morote Shuto Uke*). Step with the right foot, line 6f, into a front stance (*Zenkutsu Dachi*), and drive both open hands out to the right side of the body, allowing them to cross at the wrist, then out to the side with the palms facing away from the body to perform a middle-level block (*Shuto Kakiwake*).

Turn to face line 11 and change the stance to a horse-riding stance (*Kiba Dachi*), and drive both open hands out in front of the body, allowing them to cross at the wrist then out to the side with the palms facing towards the body to perform a middle-level block (*Haito Kakiwake*). Draw the left foot to the right foot into an informal attention stance (*Heisoku Dachi*), and lower the arms out to either side of the body into low-level blocking positions (*Ryowan Gamae*).

Turn to face line 6r and change the stance to a back stance (*Kokutsu Dachi*). At the same time, lower the left arm to a low-level blocking position and raise the right arm to a high-level blocking position (*Manji Uke*).

Turn anti-clockwise 180 degrees, line 6r, and step with the right foot into a back stance (*Kokutsu Dachi*). At the same time, lower the right arm to a low-level blocking position and raise the left arm to a high-level blocking position (*Manji Uke*). Turn anti-clockwise 180 degrees, line 6r and step with the left foot into a back stance (*Kokutsu Dachi*). At the same time, lower the left arm to a low-level blocking position and raise the right arm to a high-level blocking position (*Manji Uke*).

Turn to face line 2 and drop down on the right knee (*Kata Hiza Dachi*) and, at the same time, drive both fists downwards, allowing them to cross at the wrist, to a low-level blocking position (*Gedan Juji Uke*). Rising, step to the right with the right foot into a horse-riding stance (*Kiba Dachi*), and draw both forearms upwards, allowing them to cross at the solar plexus, then out to either side (*Ryowan Uchi Uke*).

Raise the body and change to a natural stance (*Shizentai*), and lower the arms out to either side of the body into low-level blocking positions (*Ryowan Gamae*), then draw both fists to the hips (*Ryoken Koshi Gamae*). Twisting at the waist, and allowing the knees to bend, drive around to the front with the right elbow (*Migi Hiji Barai*), and then perform the same action with the left arm (*Hidari Hiji Barai*).

Turn 180 degrees clockwise to face line 3, allowing the left foot to rest by the outside edge of the right foot (*Kosa Dachi*), and draw both forearms upwards, allowing them to cross at the solar plexus, then out to either side with the fingers directed upwards (*Naiwan Kakiwake*).

Turn the head to face line 6f and, straightening the left leg slightly, allow the left foot to move up behind the right knee (*Tsuru Ashi Dachi*). Lower the left arm to a low-level blocking position and raise the right arm to a high-level blocking position (*Manji Uke*), drive along line 6f with the outer edge of the left foot (*Hidari Yoko Geri Keage*) and, at the same time, drive the left back fist to a high-level striking position (*Hidari Jodan Uraken*), then step with the left foot, line 6f, into a front stance (*Zenkutsu Dachi*) and execute a right middle-level punch (*Migi Chudan Oi Zuki*).

Looking along line 6f, draw the right foot behind the left knee (*Tsuru Ashi Dachi*), lower the right arm to a low-level blocking position and raise the left arm to a high-level blocking position (*Manji Uke*). Draw both fists to the left hip (*Koshi Gamae*). Drive along line 6f with the outer edge of the right foot (*Migi Yoko Geri Keage*) and, at the same time, execute a right high-level back-fist strike (*Migi Jodan Uraken*), then step with the right foot into a horse-riding stance (*Kiba Dachi*) and, while drawing the right fist to the right hip, execute a left-fist strike along line 6f (*Hidari Kagi Zuki*).

Turn the head to face line 6r, and draw the left foot behind the right knee (*Tsuru Ashi Dachi*), while raising the right arm to a high-level blocking position and lowering the left arm to a low-level blocking position (*Manji Gamae*). Draw the fists to the right hip (*Koshi Gamae*), then, while driving along line 6r with the outer edge of the left foot (*Migi Yoko Geri Keage*), drive the left back fist to a high-level striking position (*Hidari Jodan Uraken*). Step with the left foot into a horse-riding stance (*Kiba Dachi*), then, while drawing the left fist to the left hip, execute a right-fist strike along line 6r (*Migi Kagi Zuki*). Draw both fists to the left hip (*Koshi Gamae*).

Turn the head to face line 6f, and drive around in an arc to the right side of the body with the right open hand (*Migi Jodan Tate Shuto Uke*). Turning the body to face line 6f, change the stance to a front stance (*Zenkutsu Dachi*), and strike the right open hand with the left elbow (*Tate Empi Uchi*).

While turning 180 degrees, line 6r, drive both open hands to a high-level position and down to the right hip (*Koshi Gamae*). At the same time, raise the left foot behind the right knee (*Tsuru Ashi Dachi*). Drive along line 6r with the outer edge of the left foot (*Hidari Yoko Geri Keage*) and, at the same time, execute a high-level left back-fist strike (*Hidari Jodan Uraken Uchi*) and lower the left foot into a front stance (*Zenkutsu Dachi*). Step with the right foot, line 6r, into a front stance (*Zenkutsu Dachi*), and execute a right middle-level punch (*Migi Chudan Oi Zuki*). Turn 180 degrees and return to *Yoi*.

6 Ten No Kata

Ten No Kata was devised by Master Funakoshi. It has two forms – *Omote* and *Ura* – and is the first step towards partner work. Although *Kata* are generally practised alone or in group formation, *Ten No Kata* introduces the student to the reality of technique. To begin with, the *Kata* is practised alone, but when the pattern of movements are learned it is practised with a partner. *Omote* means 'front' and usually refers to all the strikes made when practising alone, as the practice requires a step forward to execute the strike. *Ura* means 'back' and usually refers to work with a partner, as the practice requires a step back to defend against a strike. *Ura Ten No Kata* is the first testing ground. As one partner steps through and makes a strike, the other partner applies a blocking technique. If these techniques have been taught and learned properly the student should feel confident in both attack and defence.

In most schools, *Ten No Kata* has a total of ten strikes, five with the right hand and five with the left hand. Two of the strikes – one right (*Migi*), one left (*Hidari*) – are at low level (*Gedan*); six – three right (*Migi*), and three left (*Hidari*) – are at middle level (*Chudan*); and two – one right (*Migi*), and one left (*Hidari*) – are at high level (*Jodan*). The ten strikes are blocked using five different techniques: *Gedan Barai, Ude Uke, Uchi Komi, Shuto Uke,* and *Age Uke*. These blocking techniques are described below. The two other strikes using the back of the hand – *Haishu* – at high level – *Jodan* – are sometimes included.

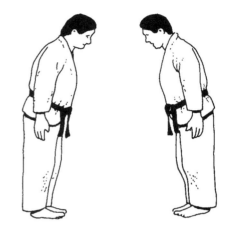

Fig 26   Bowing to each other.

The *Kata* begins with two students facing each other, at a striking distance, in *Yoi*, or 'ready' stance. As with all partner work, the students show mutual respect by bowing at the start of the *Kata* (see Fig 26). To find the correct striking distance, the students stand with outstretched arms and alter their position until their fingertips touch. A mental note is made of this distance so that it can be resumed each time an attack is made. One partner makes the first strike – usually this is mutually agreed before the *Kata* starts – by stepping forwards with the right foot into a *Zenkutsu Dachi* stance, drawing the left fist to the left hip and driving the right fist forwards in a *Gedan* (low-level) striking action. From this position the student makes the first low-level block by stepping back with the right foot into a *Zenkutsu Dachi* stance, and executing a left low-level block (*Gedan Barai*), and immediately afterwards makes a middle-level (*Chudan*) counter right-fist strike. After this, both students resume the original starting position in *Yoi* stance. The same strike, block and counter-strikes are then made from the left side, and the *Yoi* stance resumed.

It can be seen from this description of *Ten No Kata* that little space is required because there is only one step backwards for each partner, and the same starting point is resumed after each completed sequence. This is true of all five techniques – *Gedan Barai, Ude Uke, Uchi Komi, Shuto Uke, Age Uke*. By following this order the Kata can be completed: one partner executes two low-level followed by six middle-level followed by two high-level strikes, and the other partner defends using the order of blocks described above. When all the blocks and strikes have been completed, the partners exchange roles and repeat the process. This way both partners have a chance to practise blocking and striking.

All *Kata* start with the *Yoi* posture. The aim is to condition the mind so that it is ready to begin actions that have a serious implication; in other words, the attack is about to commence. The attack could come from any direction – right, left, front or rear – and a keen sense of awareness needs to be developed to sense when, and from where, the attack is coming.

The *Yoi* stance is a very important starting point. Although strong focus and awareness is required, relaxation is essential. Tension leads to rigidity and a failure to respond with good timing. Timing is critical in partner work, and in the event of an actual attack intent on inflicting bodily harm, it can make the difference between safety and untold injury.

In *Kata*, the *Yoi* stance is always assumed at the beginning and end. Because the attackers are not real, a product of the imagination and *Kata* design, it is easy to under-estimate the importance of *Yoi*. A failure to adopt a strong mental focus will lead to a weak performance and ineffective techniques. The *Yoi* positions relative to the *Kata* are described below. They are part of the important design structure of the *Kata* and should be practised diligently.

STEPPING THROUGH

So far, the act of stepping through to make a strike has been academic, but in truth it requires further discussion. In many cases, when engaged in partner work, the attacking student will make his intention clear in various ways. He might, without realizing, shift his body weight backwards, to gain momentum; or he might lean slightly forwards with his shoulders, for the same reason; his face may show more determination when the decision to strike has been made; there may be a slight pulling back of the striking fist at the hip, or a shift in position of the leading foot, and so on. Such indicators are detectable and overcome relatively quickly.

However, the more experienced student may have a degree of observation, developed through concentration, which allows him to perceive more subtle signals. Harder to eradicate, these can range from a condition in the body of the attacker to a minute movement of the eye prior to making the strike. Masters of the art are credited with a sixth sense, and are seemingly able to detect when the attack is imminent, at the same time as, or even before, it becomes a decision in the mind of the attacker.

For most practitioners, these tell-tale indicators can be dispelled by relaxing and moving from the hips and abdomen. To understand these principles fully, the student needs to experience them in the presence of an experienced and revealing teacher. They are without doubt the most important aspects of body movement and condition.

Partners need to help each other as much as possible by giving information about what is seen and felt. If this is done, the attacker develops a more natural way of stepping, and the defender develops a much keener sense of awareness. A common error in this practice is to get into a rhythm. The mind adjusts naturally to rhythm and, if the strike and counter become regular, the student may be deceived about how well he is anticipating strikes. After each strike and counter students should pause, gain composure, relax, then strike without hesitation. The length of the pauses should be irregular, from a few seconds to possibly minutes. This will prevent rhythm, and the practice will depend on concentration rather than competition and habit.

Partner work should give equal benefit to both partners; studying a partner, helping to overcome weaknesses, and learning from them, will lead to mutual development. Once weaknesses are overcome in partner work, and the technique understood, the development needs to be transferred to *Kata* practice. The techniques should become sharper and cleaner, precise and elegant, both to watch and perform. It is essential to understand the reason why something works, as it is not always possible to have a partner to work with. Technique involves form, body posture, movement, weight transference, focus and mental application. If these elements are transferred into a regular routine of practice, the *Kata* will gain impetus, and the practitioner, by realizing his potential, will gain a deeper insight into the art.

MAAI - TIMING AND DISTANCE

Maai means 'spatial distance' and has come to include the sense of timing. To everything there is a time and a season. Being in the right place at the right time is a knack that seems to be innate in some people, but most need to work at understanding and mastering it. This is especially true in the martial arts. Being in the wrong place at the wrong time can be devastating.

Timing and distance require understanding that can only come through practice. If a defender is within striking distance and the attacker makes a strike, then the defender must move or be struck. However, moving out of reach of the attack is only a basic answer to understanding timing and distance. It is when the movement is made that is crucially important. When the attacker makes a strike, even if he is holding a knife or a sledgehammer, if the defender is out of reach he cannot be harmed. If the defender moves too soon, however, the attacker will be aware of this and quickly make a second strike; and if the defender makes another move too soon, defeat is bound to follow.

The defender's movement has to be at the right time. The attacker must feel confident that he has been successful. For this to happen, the defender must leave minimum space between himself and the attacker's strike. In many ways, this is a courageous act. If the defender gets the timing wrong, the attacker's success is sure.

Even if the defender moves at the right time, if he mis-judges the distance he will still lose to the attacker. Timing, therefore, requires accurate judgement of distance. The defender needs to know precisely whether the attacker can reach his target, and needs to be able to move to within that distance if required. The difficulties of timing and distance are clearer, as is the need for a practice to develop a mastery of them.

There are different ways of effecting this sort of practice, but the aim is always the same. *Ten No Kata* is an excellent practice for timing and distance. The initial benefit of this *Kata* is that both partners know what is about to happen – the techniques remain the same, the power and precision of the attacks remain the same –they can, therefore, devote the whole of the practice to timing and distance. One element of surprise does remain, however – when the attack is to be made. This is the responsibility of both partners. The attacker must do all he can to disguise his intention, and the defender must concentrate very hard to detect the attacker's intention. This practice has the effect of sharpening the ability to anticipate an attack. An inability to anticipate attack makes response slow and defence very difficult. Once this ability is developed, the distance required can be calculated precisely. If the defender is as close as possible to the attack, without it having any effect, the attacker thinks he is

successful. In a real situation the attacker would be stunned to see that his attack was ineffective, making him hesitate and giving the edge to the defender.

Ten No Kata is a deceptively simple practice. Two partners who practise together all the time will tend not to see their progress. The more the attack is disguised, the sharper the perception of the defender has to be. Initial progress is fast but, as time passes, the situation becomes more difficult to read. When a degree of competence has been gained, working with an inexperienced partner feels like slow motion, as the attacker signals too much and the attack is too slow, giving the defender all the time he needs to calculate his timing and distance. This will also give the beginner a false sense of the defender's speed. The defender will seem to be moving very quickly, when in fact it is his mental response that is fast. However, changing partners among practitioners who have developed a high degree of proficiency will have a beneficial effect, making the attacker and defender think even more seriously about what they are doing. Everyone is different and, although the practice is identical for everyone, responses and intentions vary considerably. Two partners working together all the time will become accustomed to each other. Changing partners helps to add an essential unpredictable element, which will always be evident in a real attack, where the intention is to cause actual bodily harm.

7 Sparring Techniques

SAMBON KUMITE - THREE-STEP SPARRING

When the techniques are well practised in *Ten No Kata*, students progress to basic sparring. Unlike *Ten No Kata*, where one backward step is required, basic sparring involves three or more steps. This introduces the student to a progression of attacks that require good judgement in timing and distance. As with the start of *Ten No Kata*, two students stand facing each other, and show their respect by bowing. The student defending remains in the *Yoi* posture, and the student attacking steps back into a front stance. The attacker takes three steps forwards and with each step delivers a middle-level punch. The defender, in rhythm with the attacker, takes three steps backwards and with each step blocks the attacker's punch. On the third punch, the defender blocks and makes a counter. Both students then return to the *Yoi* posture. The students then exchange roles – the defender becomes the attacker and the attacker becomes the defender – and three steps are made in the other direction with the relevant blocks and strikes being performed. By exchanging roles, the students have equal training in both attack and defence.

GOHON KUMITE - FIVE STEP SPARRING

In effect, this is the same as three-step sparring but involves five steps instead of three. The advantage of five-step sparring is that the student can critically test timing and distance. The defender chooses any one of the five attacks against which to make a counter and stop the attacker. Neither the defender nor the attacker knows when the counter will be made – it may be against the first or any one of the remaining four. The decision to make the counter is spontaneous. The defender must feel confident with the timing and distance to make the block and counter effective. The attacker must make all five attacks positive to add realism to the defender's response. The aim is to block well before the attack is complete and the attacker has 'confirmed' in the stance. If this is not achieved, when the pace quickens, the defender will be unsuccessful.

IPPON KUMITE - SINGLE ENGAGEMENT MATCHES

With *Gohon* and *Sambon Kumite* the direction is a straight line. The object of *Ippon Kumite* is to practise techniques while moving in all directions. The fundamental importance of this type of sparring is to accustom the mind to looking for 'openings' in the partner's defence; to be able to strike without signalling the intent to do so, and to retreat quickly once the attack has been made. The defender, on the other hand, tries hard to sense when an attack is imminent, and block it before it makes contact.

Initially, the sparring match may be pre-arranged so that one partner makes all the attacks and the other defends, then the partners exchange roles. The attacker may even call out the level of the attack to warn the defender. (At this stage, the strikes are mainly middle level for safety reasons.) As students become more competent the call is omitted.

IRIMI

Irimi is the art of avoiding an attack by stepping into and very slightly to the side of the attack. At high speed this takes a little courage, and is usually practised by higher-grade students. The advantage of this practice is that timing and distance can be perfected. *Irimi* is used in a variety of practices. In *Ten No Kata*, *Irimi* is used to heighten the sense of anticipation, the feeling of 'knowing' when the attack is about to be made, and responding accordingly. In three- or five-step sparring, *Irimi* is used to test timing, distance, and the ability to change direction successfully at high speed.

JIYU KUMITE – FREE-STYLE SPARRING

Ten No Kata, three- and five-step sparring, and *Irimi* are all precursors to free-style sparring. This practice is sometimes abused by students and practitioners who interpret the word 'free' to mean 'anything goes'. Free-style sparring represents an opportunity for the student to test all the techniques learned in *Kihon* and *Kata*. This practice can only be successfully performed by students who respect each other and are willing to provide feedback on well-timed and well-executed techniques. True free-style sparring is non-competitive, adding impetus and a degree of realism to the practice of *Kata*. It is in free-style sparring that the character of the student shows. Impetuous and over-zealous students are carried away and the practice becomes a match of daring and risk. Bruising, and even the spilling of blood, can result from temper and lack of control, little progress is made, interest in the art fades and students drift away. With a good attitude, however, considerable progress is made; techniques are executed well, enjoyment and interest are increased, and a competent, unassuming manner develops. The mind adapts to speed, and is continually tested.

If students obey some basic rules or guidelines, the all-round practice of karate-do should be fulfilling. In his book *Karate-Do Kyohan*, the Master says that sparring should be practised to improve *Kata*, in other words, sparring is a testing ground for all those splendid techniques learned in *Kata*. If a technique fails in sparring it is because it failed in *Kata*. *Kata* is the soul of karate and an impure soul gains little of lasting value.

8 A–Z of Kata Techniques

Fig 27 Age Uke.

AGE UKE

Rising block. Draw the right arm across the stomach so the fist is in alignment with the left side of the chest, the palm facing upwards. Continue by driving the fist upwards in alignment with the left side of the chest and face until the arm is 6in (15cm) above the head. At this point, allow the fist to turn anti-clockwise until the palm is directed away from the body and drive the fist forwards 6in (15cm). Bending at the wrist, allow the fist to turn upwards so the knuckle of the index finger is pointing directly above.

AGE ZUKI

Rising strike. This is a high-level strike. Drive forwards with the right fist, with the

Fig 28 Age Zuki.

fingers facing upwards and the elbow tucked into the body. As the striking fist goes forward, the inside of the upper right arm should skim past the right side of the chest. At the end of the strike, allow the fist to turn anti-clockwise in a semi-circle until the fingers are directed downwards.

BASSAI DAI POSTURE

Stand with the feet together and the knees slightly bent. The back must remain straight, with the posterior pushed in. The hands are brought together just in front of the groin. The right hand forms a fist, with the fingers towards the abdomen. The left open hand covers the fingers of the right hand and the thumbs of both hands are touching. The fingers and the back of the right hand are cupped in the palm of the left hand and the left fingers cover the knuckles on the right hand and lie half-way across the back of the hand. The arms are slightly bent, the armpits closed and the hands about 4in (10cm) away from the lower stomach. The elbows should be tucked in to the ribs on either side.

CHUDAN ZUKI

Middle-level strike.

Fig 29   Bassai Dai Posture.

Fig 30   Chudan Zuki.

EMPI POSTURE

Stand with the feet together. Move the left open hand to the left hip with the palm facing towards the body. The inside of the left wrist should be touching the base of the ribs on the left side. Take the right fist to the left hand, with the knuckles touching the palm, and the fingers of the right hand facing the abdomen. The inside of the right wrist should just be touching the abdomen and the left elbow should be tucked into the body. The fingers and thumb of the left hand should be pressed together so that the hand forms a straight line.

EMPI

Elbow strike. This elbow strike is made by driving the right elbow back to strike at an opponent attacking from the rear.

Fig 31   Empi.

EMPI UCHI

Elbow strike. Make sure the arm does not obscure the vision.

Fig 32   Empi Uchi.

EMPI UKE

Elbow block. Here, the elbow is used to block an attack coming from the side. With the fists resting on the hips and the elbows directed out to either side, the body is twisted forwards and the outside edge of the elbow is used to make the block.

Fig 33   Empi Uke.

Fig 34   Fumikomi.

FUMIKOMI

Stamping. This is a stamping strike made by drawing the right knee up to the chest, with the lower part of the leg directed downwards. Draw the toes back and drive downwards towards the attacker's leg. Keep the body upright and facing forwards until the strike is about to make contact, then, allowing the body to turn slightly to the left, twist on the ball of the left foot to a 45-degree angle and point the outer edge of the right foot downwards so that the sole is facing the floor. At the point of contact, and while turning on the ball of the left foot, drop the body weight by bending the left knee.

GEDAN BARAI

Low-level sweeping block. While in a right front stance, raise the right fist to the left shoulder with the fingers to the side of the face. Drive the back of the fist down to a point about 6in (15cm) above the right knee. When this point is reached, allow the fist to turn clockwise so the fingers are facing the knee.

GEDAN GAMAE

Low-level posture. This posture is very similar to *Gedan Barai* but in a shorter stance.

GEDAN SHUTO UKE

Low-level knife-hand block. Here the knife-hand strike or block is used by sweeping around in a low stance and striking at low level.

Fig 36   Gedan Barai.

Fig 37   Gedan Gamae.

Fig 38   Gedan Shuto Uke.

Fig 39   Gankamu Gamae.

GANKAKU GAMAE

Crane on a rock posture. Stand on the right foot with the knee bent, and draw the left foot just behind the right knee. The right arm is raised in an 'L' shape and the left arm is in a low-level blocking position.

GYAKU HANMI

Reverse half-facing. This is similar to Zenkutsu Dachi with the body twisted at the waist towards the forward leg – in this example, the right shoulder is turned towards the extended left leg. It is usually performed in conjunction with a block.

Fig 40   Gyaku Hanmi.

Fig 41   Gyaku Zuki.

Fig 42   Haishu Awaze Uke.

GYAKU ZUKI

Reverse strike. Stepping forwards into a left front stance, drive the right fist forwards to make a middle-level punch. The fist should drive forwards with the fingers facing upwards and the elbow tucked into the body. As the striking fist goes forwards the inside of the upper right arm should skim past the right side of the chest. At the end of the strike, allow the fist to turn anti-clockwise until the fingers are directed downwards.

HAISHU AWASE UKE

Back hand combined block. Raise the hands to head height, and position them back to back. The fingers should be directed upwards and almost in alignment.

HAISHU JUJI UKE

Back hand crossed block. This block may be performed at high or low level. For example, drive both open hands upwards and forwards, allowing them to cross at the

Fig 43   Haishu Juji Uke.

Fig 44   Haishu Uke.

wrist with the right wrist resting on the left. The hands should be slightly above head height and driving forwards.

HAISHU UKE

Back hand block. Drive the left open hand around to the left of the body until the arm is outstretched. The thumb edge of the hand should be directed to the rear, and the back of the hand is used to make the block.

HAITO IPPON KEN

Ridge-hand one-knuckle fist. Draw the fists up to the chest with the elbows directed out to either side and the knuckle of the first finger protruding. Drive both fists out to the front as if striking at the nipples of the opponent with the knuckles of the first fingers.

Fig 45   Haito Ippon Ken.

Fig 46   Haito Kakiwake.

HAITO KAKIWAKE

Ridge-hand wedging. Move the open hands across the body until they cross at the solar plexus. The inside of the right forearm should be just in front of the outside of the left forearm and the fingers of the hands should be facing away to either side of the body. Continue moving the arm upwards and forwards and allow them to separate at about shoulder height. Keep the elbows bent and close to the chest. Bring the right hand in line with the right shoulder and the left hand in line with the left shoulder. At this point, allow the hands to turn, the right in a clockwise direction and the left in an anti-clockwise direction, until the fingers are directed upwards and slightly forwards, and the palms are directed towards the body.

Fig 47   Haito Uke (i).

Fig 48   Haito Uke (ii).

HAITO UKE (I)

Ridge-hand block. Lower the right arm to a low-level blocking position. Draw the left open hand across the chest so that the thumb edge of the hand is resting by the right upper arm. The fingers should be directed away to the right side and the palm facing downwards.

HAITO UKE (II)

Ridge-hand block. The thumb edge of the hand is used to make the block by sweeping the hand from one side of the body to the other in a semi-circle.

HAIWAN UKE

Back arm block. Raise the left arm out to the left side of the body, bent at the elbow, with the forearm directed upwards, and the thumb edge of the fist directed towards the face.

HANGETSU DACHI

Hour-glass stance. This is referred to as the hour-glass stance because it is concave at the knees and the body shape resembles the outline of an hour-glass. Take a step forwards with the right foot. Turn the right foot by pivoting on the ball of the foot until the outer edge of the foot is

Fig 49   Haiwan Uke.

horizontal to the starting point. Test this stance by drawing an imaginary line from the left heel to the right heel, then, following the line of the toes, draw another two lines until they meet. This should produce a triangle of space. Bend the knees inwards towards each other until the thighs are almost vertically aligned.

HANMI KAESHI DORI

Half-facing counter. This technique is performed by sweeping the open hand upwards under the attacker's arm, grasping hold, twisting, then pulling the arm down slightly.

Fig 50   Hangetsu Dachi.

Fig 51   Hanmi Kaeshi Dori.

HANMI SASHI ASHI

Half-facing balance leg. This is a half-facing stepping movement requiring smoothness and balance. One foot is passed across and parallel to the other.

HEISOKU DACHI

Attention stance. This is a simple stance. The feet are drawn together so the inside edges of each foot are touching. The body is upright, relaxed, and ready for action.

Fig 52   Hanmi Sashi Ashi.

Fig 53   Heisoku Dachi.

HIJI BARAI

Elbow sweeping block. Draw both fists to the hips with the elbows directed out to the sides, akimbo. Rotate the body forwards and use the elbow to block a strike coming to the front of the body. Allow the body to twist.

Fig 54   Hiji Barai.

Fig 55   Hiza Gamae.

HIZA GAMAE

Knee posture. Drive the knee upwards and forwards until it is in line with the lower chest. The toes should be pointing downwards, and there should be a strong feeling of balance.

HIZA UCHI

Knee strike. Drive the knee upwards and forwards until it is level with the upper part of the chest. The lower part of the leg and the foot should be directed downwards. At the same time as the right leg rises, reach forwards and upwards with the hands, palms facing each other, until they

Fig 56 Hiza Uchi.

Fig 57 Jiai No Kamae.

are above head height and stretched out in front of you. At the point of contact, draw the hands down vertically past the knee and to the sides of the lower leg.

JIAI NO KAMAE

Affection, kindness, love. This is the starting posture for *Jion* and *Jutte* and is described in the *Jion Kata*.

JODAN SHUTO UCHI

High-level knife-hand strike. The movement for this technique is the same as for Age Uke but with the hand open.

Fig 58 Jodan Shuto Uchi.

JODAN MOROTE UKE

High-level two-hands block. Draw the right fist towards the left hip and drive upwards to the right side of the body to above head height. At the same time, support the right arm with the left fist positioned just below the left elbow. The thumb edge of the left fist should be directed forwards.

JOHO KAITEN TOBI

Jumping turning kick. In Fig 60 the jump is made while turning through 360 degrees. Step with the right foot into a front stance. Pushing the body weight back on to the left leg, leap high into the air and make a 360-degree turn, drawing the knees up to the chest and landing, quietly, into a back stance with the right foot forward.

Fig 59   Jodan Morote Uke.

Fig 60   Joho Kaiten Tobi.

JUJI UKE

Crossed block. Step forwards into a front stance and drive both fists downwards and forwards, allowing them to cross at the wrist with the right wrist resting on the left. The wrists should be positioned about 9 or 10in (22-25cm) from the leading knee, with the fingers facing downwards. The body must remain upright.

Fig 61   Juji Uke.

KAESHI DORI

Attached palm hand catch. Effectively this is like drawing the right palm upwards under the arm of the attacker and, having grasped hold, twisting the arm and pulling it downwards.

Fig 62   Kaeshi Dori.

KAGI GAMAE

Hooking posture. Draw the left fist to the left hip, and the right arm across the chest. The fist of the right arm should be level with the left side of the ribs with the fingers directed downward. There should be a 4 to 5-in gap between the arm and the chest.

Fig 64   Kagi Zuki.

Fig 63   Kagi Gamae.

KAGI ZUKI

Hooking strike. The positioning for this technique is similar to that of *Kagi Gamae* but with the intention of using the right fist to make a strike. Allow the fist to drive further out to the side of the body than in *Kagi Gamae.*

Fig 65   Kaishu Haiwan Uke.

KAISHU HAIWAN UKE

Open-hand back arm block. Raise the left open hand out to the left side of the body with the arm bent upwards in an 'L' shape. The back of the hand should be directed away to the rear of the body, and the elbow angled away to the left.

KAISHU HAIWAN UKE

This is the same as the movement in Fig 65.

KAISHU KOSA UKE

Open-hand crossed block. Step forwards into a front stance. Drive the right open hand upwards with the fingers directed forwards and the palm facing upwards. The right arm should be in a 'V' shape with the armpit closed. At the same time, drive the left open hand downwards with the fingers directed forwards and the palm facing downwards. While performing this action, allow the arms to cross at the abdomen.

Fig 66   Kaishu Haiwan Uke.

Fig 67   Kaishu Kosa Uke.

KAISHU RYOWAN GAMAE

Open-hand both arms posture. Rotate the arms in large counter-circles above the head, lowering and crossing at the chest and then out to the sides. The hands should be open and the palms directed towards the feet. The hands should be about 12-15in (30-35cm) away from the sides of the body.

KAISHU YAMA GAMAE

Open-hand mountain posture. This is sometimes referred to as the mountain posture. Raise the arms in counter semi-circles to the sides of the body, each bent at the elbow in 'L'-shaped right angles, with the fingers directed upwards and the palms directed towards each other.

Fig 68   Kaishu Ryowan Gamae.

Fig 69   Kaishu Yama Gamae.

KAKE DORI

Hooked catch. Having drawn the hand up and under the wrist of the attacker, allow it to turn over so the palm is directed downwards, as if twisting the wrist against the joint.

right shoulder and the left fist in line with the left shoulder. At this point, allow the fists to turn, the right in an anti-clockwise direction and the left in a clockwise direction, until the fingers are directed forwards away from the body.

Fig 70   Kake Dori.

Fig 71   Kakiwake Uke.

KAKIWAKE UCHI

Wedging block. Move the fists across the body until they cross at the solar plexus. The inside of the right forearm should be just in front of the outside of the left forearm and the fingers of the fists should be facing the body. Continue moving the arms upwards and forwards and allow them to separate at about shoulder height. Keep the elbows bent and close to the chest. Bring the right fist in line with the

KAMI ZUKAMI

Hair on head grab handfull. Having made a high-level strike, *Jodan Zuki*, allow the hand to open in preparation for grasping the opponent's hair.

KATA HIZA DACHI

Form knee stance. This technique involves dropping down on to one knee while performing a technique.

Fig 72   Kami Zukami.

KANKU DAI POSTURE

To look at the sky. Stand with feet shoulder-width apart and toes pointing forwards. Bring the hands together about 12in (30cm) in front of the lower abdomen. With the hands open and the fingers straight, allow the left first and second fingertips to cover the right first and second fingertips. All the fingers are pressed together. Extend the thumbs away from the hand towards the body in a parallel position, and allow them to touch at the tips. There should now be a triangular space between the thumbs and first fingers.

Fig 73   Kata Hiza Dachi.

Fig 74   Kanku Dai Posture.

The arms are slightly bent, the armpits closed and the open hands pointing downwards to a point on the floor about 3ft from the body. The shoulders are relaxed.

KATAASHI DACHI

Form leg stance. While standing on the left leg, draw the top of the right foot behind the left leg to a point just above the calf muscle. There should be a strong feeling of balance.

KIBA DACHI

Horse-riding stance. This stance is referred to as the horse-riding stance because the positioning of the legs is similar to that adopted when riding a horse. To achieve the correct positioning, stand with the feet together, then turn the feet outwards so the toes are facing 35 degrees to the sides; push the heel out to the side until they are facing 35 degrees away from the body to the rear, and once again turn the feet so the toes are pointing 35 degrees away from the body. Finally, slowly push the heel out to the side until the outside edge of each foot is parallel to the other – the toes are facing forwards in a straight line. At this point, allow the knees to bend as if sitting down. The height of the stance is about that of a normal sitting position. The posterior should not protrude. The body weight should be supported by the feet rather than by the knees.

Fig 75   Kataashi Dachi.

Fig 76   Kiba Dachi.

KIN GERI

Testes kick. Draw the right knee up towards the chest until the thigh is almost parallel to the floor, and the lower part of the leg is in a vertical position. Press the toes downwards and, pivoting at the knee, drive the top of the foot forwards until the leg is almost straight and the foot is at groin height. At the end of the strike, allow the lower part of the leg to return to its vertical position – knee chest high, the thigh parallel to the floor, and the lower part of the leg in a vertical position – then lower it to the floor into a front stance.

Fig 77   Kin Geri

KOHO TSUKI AGE

Back direction rising thrust. While standing in *Shizentai,* drive the right fist upwards past the right side of the face, supported by the left fist at the right elbow. This is a strike to the chin of an opponent standing behind.

Fig 78   Koho Tsuki Age.

KOKUTSU DACHI

Back bent leg stance. See Fig 22 for positioning of the feet. The body is turned sideways but with the head still looking forward; the body weight is moved over the back leg rather than the front and the heels are in alignment. The front foot is facing forward and the rear foot is angled at 45 degrees. Keep the body upright.

Fig 79   Kokutsu Dachi.

Fig 80   Kosa Dachi.

KOSA DACHI

Crossed stance. Stepping with the right leg forward in stance, draw the left foot towards and to the outside edge of the right foot. The right foot should be firmly planted, and the ball of the left foot should be touching the floor with the heel raised and the foot angled towards the outside edge of the right foot.

KOSA UKE

Crossed block. Raise the right fist to the left

shoulder with the back of the fist to the face and the elbow close to the chest. Drive forwards in a diagonal line from left to right until the fist is level with the right shoulder and in line with the right knee. The arm should be bent at the elbow in a 'V' shape. When this point is reached, allow the fist to turn clockwise until the palm is facing upwards. At the same time, raise the left fist to the right shoulder, palm to the side of the face. Drive the back of the fist down to a low-level blocking position. When this point is reached, allow the fist to turn clockwise so the palm is facing downwards.

Fig 81   Kosa Uke.

Fig 81(a)   Kosa Uke.

KOSHI GAMAE

Hip posture. Draw the left fist to the left hip with the fingers facing upwards. The little finger edge of the forearm should be resting against the lower left ribs. Maintain this left arm position and draw the right fist to the left fist so the little finger edge of the right fist is touching the upward-facing fingers of the left hand.

Fig 82   Koshi Gamae.

MAE EMPI

Front elbow. This is an elbow strike to defend against attack from the front, used here to strike the palm of the left hand.

Fig 83   Mae Empi.

MAE GERI

Front kick. Step forwards into a left front stance. Draw the right knee up towards the chest until the thigh is parallel to the floor, and the lower part of the leg is in a vertical position. Draw the toes back and, pivoting at the knee, drive the ball of the foot forwards until the leg is almost straight. At the end of the strike, allow the lower part of the leg to return to its vertical position – knee chest high , thigh parallel to the floor, and the lower part of the leg in a vertical position – then lower it to the floor into a front stance.

Fig 83   Mae Geri

4-5ft

Fig 84   Mae Tobi Geri.

MAE TOBI GERI

Front jumping kick. Step forwards into a right front stance. While leaping upwards and forwards, draw the left knee up towards the chest until the thigh is parallel to the floor, springing from the right leg. During the leap the left thigh is parallel to the floor and the lower part of the leg is in a vertical position. Drive forwards with the right foot, drawing the toes back and, pivoting at the knee, drive the ball of the foot forwards until the leg is almost straight. At the end of the strike, drop on the balls of the feet into a right front stance. The landing should be as quiet as possible, with both feet landing at the same time.

MANJI GAMAE

Swastika posture. Allow the arms to cross

Fig 85   Manji Gamae

by the solar plexus parallel to each other, then raise the left arm up to the left side of the body in a high-level block in an 'L' shape, and the right arm into a right low-level block. The left arm is angled to 45 degrees with the palm of the fist facing to the back of the head. The attention is focused on the right low-level block.

MANJI UKE

The positioning for this is the same as for *Manji Gamae*, but with the intention of blocking.

MIKAZUKI

Crescent moon. This is often referred to as a crescent moon kick because of the semi-circular motion. Raise the knee to the side until it is level with the hip. The extended leg should be bent at the knee to form an angle, and the lower leg should be sloping downwards to the rear. To keep your balance, allow the body to lean slightly to the left. Drive the knee forwards and allow the lower part of the leg to swing outwards and around to the front, with the toes pointing upwards and the sole of the foot angled to the left.

Fig 86   Manji Uke.

Fig 87   Mikazuki.

115

MIKAZUKI GERI

Crescent moon strike. The action for this is the same as for *Mikazuki* but a strike is made to the opposite open hand.

MIZUNAGARE NO KAMAE

Water flowing posture. This refers to the positioning of the right or left arm across the chest that is angled down slightly.

Fig 88   Mizunagare No Kamae.

MOROTE AGE UKE

Two-hands rising block. This is like performing two *Age Uke* at the same time but with the knuckles of the fists touching and the palms directed away from the body.

Fig 89   Morote Age Uke.

MOROTE JO DORI

Both hands Jo staff catch. This is a Jo staff technique. Draw the right foot to the inside of the left knee. The ball of the foot should be making contact with the left inside knee. Raise the right arm out to the right side of the body in an 'L' shape, with the fist lightly closed. Draw the left arm across the abdomen so the fist is in alignment with the right elbow and the fist lightly closed. The left fist and right arm should be in alignment as if holding a Jo staff vertically.

Fig 90   Morote Jo Dori.

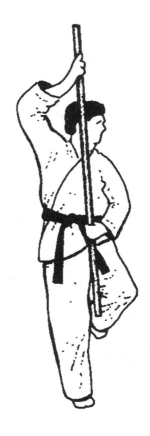

Fig 91   Morote Jo Dori.

MOROTE JO TSUKI DASHI

Two-hands Jo staff thrusting stance. This is a technique involving the Jo staff. Stepping into a front stance, drive both open hands forwards – the right at high level and the left at middle level – as if to be grasping hold of the Jo staff.

MOROTE JO UKE

Two-hands Jo staff block. The posture for this is the same as for *Morote Jo Tsuki Dashi* but with the intention of taking the Jo staff from an opponent.

MOROTE KOKO DORI

Both hands tiger mouth catch. The posture for this is the same as for *Morote Jo Uke*. Here the position of the hands is exchanged by rotating them, as if rotating the Jo staff.

MOROTE KOKO GAMAE

Both hands tiger mouth posture. Reach

Fig 92   Moroto Jo Tsuki Dashi.

Fig 94   Morote Koko Dori.

Fig 93   Morote Jo Uke.

Fig 95   Morote Koko Gamae.

Fig 96   Morote Kubi Osae.

Fig 97   Morote Uke.

out to high level with the left open hand with the fingers directed to the right. Reach out to low level with the left open hand with the fingers directed downwards. The intention here is to grasp the opponent by the throat and lower part of the body and, by rotating the hand positions, throw the opponent off balance.

MOROTE KUBI OSAE

Two-hands neck pressing. Reach upwards and forwards with both open hands to head height. Both arms should be outstretched, with the palms facing downwards and the fingers pointing slightly towards each other. The space between each hand should be the same as the width of the head. (The intention here is to grab the attacker's head or the collar on either side.)

MOROTE UKE

Two-hands block. This block is very similar to *Ude Uke*. Raise the right fist to the left shoulder with the back of the fist to the face and the elbow close to the chest. Drive forwards in a diagonal line from left to right until the fist is level with the right shoulder. The arm should be bent at the elbow in a 'V' shape. When this point is reached, allow the fist to turn clockwise until the palm is facing upwards. While performing this action, draw the left fist to the right elbow, to the side and just behind the elbow joint, with the fingers of the left fist directed upwards. The left fist is intended to support the right blocking arm.

MOROTE YOKO KEN ATE

Two-hands side fist strike. Here the fists

Fig 98   Morote Yoko Ken Ate.

Fig 99   Morote Zuki.

are drawn to the chest, with the elbows directed out to the side, and the knuckle of the index fingers protruding in preparation to make a double forward strike to the opponent's nipples.

MOROTE ZUKI

Two-hands strike. Draw both fists to the right hip with the fingers facing upwards. Drive both fists out to the left side of the body. The right arm should be positioned across the chest and in line with the left shoulder, and the left arm should be extended with the palm of the fist directed downwards.

MOTO DACHI

Resulting stance. This is a stance resulting from twisting the body while performing a technique.

NAGASHI UKE

Sweeping block. Extend the left fist out to the front of the body to a low-level blocking position. Sweep the right arm out to the right side of the body and slightly to the rear, with the forearm vertically aligned – in an 'L' shape – and the fingers of the right hand directed towards the left side of the body.

Fig 100   Moto Dachi.

Fig 101   Nagashi Uke.

NAGASHI UKE

Sweeping block. This sweeping block is used by drawing the left arm across the chest as if sweeping away a middle-level strike.

Fig 102   Nagashi Uke.

NAIWAN KAKIWAKE

Forearm wedging block. Move the fists across the body until they cross at the solar plexus. The inside of the right forearm should be just in front of the outside of the left forearm and the fingers of the fists should be facing away to either side of the body. Continue moving the arm upwards and forwards and allow them to separate at

121

Fig 103   Naiwan Kakiwake.

Fig 104   Nami Ashi.

about shoulder height. Keep the elbows bent and close to the chest. Bring the right fist in line with the right shoulder and the left fist in line with the left shoulder. At this point, allow the fists to turn, the right in an anti-clockwise direction and the left in a clockwise direction, until the palms are directed towards the body.

NAMI ASHI

Returning wave leg. An avoidance or a block. Assume a horse-riding stance. Look to the left. Quickly draw the left foot to a point just above and in front of the right thigh, then step back into a horse-riding stance. At the point where the left foot reaches the right thigh, the sole of the foot should be directed upwards.

NEKO ASHI DACHI

Cat-leg stance. Also sometimes called the cat stance, this stance resembles the posture of a cat about to pounce on its prey. See Fig 24 for positioning the feet. All the body weight is supported by the right leg. Bend the right knee slightly. Resting on the ball of the left foot, turn the raised heel towards the instep of the right foot. The left toes should now be directed forwards and the heel of the left foot directed towards the right instep. Remember to keep the body upright.

OI ZUKI

Lounge punch. Step into a right front stance, draw the left fist to the left hip with the

Fig 105   Neko Ashi Dachi.

fingers directed upwards, and drive for-wards with the right fist. The fist should drive forwards, with the fingers facing upwards and the elbow tucked into the body. As the striking fist goes forwards, the inside of the upper right arm should skim past the right side of the chest. At the end of the strike, allow the fist to turn anti-clock-wise in a semi-circle until the fingers are directed downwards.

OSAE UKE

Pressing block. Raise the left open hand forwards and upwards to a point about 12in (30cm) in front of the left side of the face, with the palm facing to the right. Keep the elbow tucked into the chest. The arm should now be in a vertical 'V' shape with the fingers pointing upwards. Pivoting on the elbow, allow the left hand

Fig 106   Oi Zuki.

Fig 107   Osae Uke.

palm to lower until the fingertips are level with the right side of the chest and in line with the abdomen. The arm should be sloping down to the right slightly.

OTOSHI UKE

Dropping block. Using the forearm and fist, raise the right arm upwards above the head and towards the rear, with the fingers directed forwards. Drive the right fist and forearm downwards to a point about 8in (20cm) in front of the abdomen. At this point the right arm should be positioned horizontally.

OTOSHI ZUKI

Dropping strike. Raise the right fist high above the head and drive downwards to about groin level.

REINOJI DACHI

'L' stance. Standing with the feet together, turn the left foot 45 degrees to the left. The heels should be touching and the feet at right-angles to each other.

RYOKEN KOSHI GAMAE

Both fists hip posture. Draw both fists to

Fig 108   Otoshi Uke.

Fig 109   Otoshi Zuki.

Fig 110   Reinoji Dachi.

the hips with the fingers directed away from the rear of the body and the elbows directed out to the left and right sides, akimbo.

RYUSUI NO KAMAE

Flowing water. The positioning for this is the same as for *Mizunagare No Kamae* but with the hand open and the palm facing downwards.

RYO HIJI HARAI AGE

Both elbows sweeping rising. This is a rising block performed by strongly drawing both fists up to the chest with the fingers directed downwards. The thumb edges of the fists should be 3-4in (8-10cm) from the nipples. The elbows should be directed out to either side of the body.

Fig 111   Ryoken Koshi Gamae.

Fig 112   Ryusui No Kamae.

Fig 113   Ryo Hiji Harai Age.

RYOTE FUSE

Both hands face down.

RYO UDE MAWASHI UKE

Both arms round-house block. This is similar to the raised arm in *Manji Uke*, with the intention of blocking an attack from the side or to the rear.

Fig 114   Ryote Fuse.

*Fig 114(a)
Ryote Fuse.*

Fig 115   Ryo Ude Mawashi Uke.

Fig 116   Ryowan Gamae.

RYOWAN GAMAE

Both arms posture. Rotate both arms in complete circles past the face and body, the left arm in a clockwise direction, and the right arm in an anti-clockwise direction. The arms should cross by the face and drive downwards and outwards until they are level with the hips on either side of the body. The hands are closed with the palms facing towards the hips and there should be about 12in (30cm) of space between each palm and the hips.

RYOWAN GEDAN KAKIWAKE

Both arms low-level wedging. The action for this technique is the same as for *Ryowan Gamae* but with the intention of opening or driving an attacking low-level strike out to the side.

Fig 117   Ryowan Gedan Kakiwake.

Fig 118   *Ryowan Uchi Uke.*

Fig 119   *Sagi Ashi Dachi.*

RYOWAN UCHI UKE

Both arms striking block. The action for this is the same as for *Kakiwake Uchi* with the palms of the fists directed towards the face; the outer forearms make the blocking action.

SAGI ASHI DACHI

Heron leg stance. Keeping the left knee bent slightly, draw the right foot to the inside of the left knee. The ball of the foot should be making contact with the left inside knee.

SHIHON NUKITE

Four-finger spear hand. Drive forwards with the right open hand with the thumb edge facing upwards and the palm facing to the left. The thumb and fingers should be

Fig 120   *Shihon Nukite.*

Fig 120(a)   Shihon Nukite.

Fig 122   Shuto Kakiwake.

Fig 121   Shizentai.

pressed together and the strike is made at middle level. This is often supported by the back of the left hand under the right elbow.

SHIZENTAI

Natural posture. *Shizentai* is not really a posture or stance, but more of a relaxed and natural body condition while standing.

SHUTO KAKIWAKE

Knife-hand wedging. The arms position for this technique is the same as that for *Kakiwake Uchi* but with the hands open and the palms directed away from the body.

SHUTO GEDAN BARAI

Knife-hand low-level sweeping. Basically this is the same as *Gedan Barai* but with the hand open. Here the technique is performed in a very low form of *Kokutsu*

Fig 123   Shuto Gedan Barai.

Fig 124   Shuto Jodan Uchi.

Dachi. The left leg is forward, the body is low. The left open hand is level with and just above the left leg, and the right open hand is level with the solar plexus, with the little finger edge just touching the abdomen.

SHUTO JODAN UCHI

Knife-hand high-level strike. Raise the open hand to the side of the head and drive forwards and slightly in a curve to the neck of the attacker. The little finger edge is used to make contact and the palm is directed upwards.

SHUTO JUJI UKE

Knife-hand crossed block. Step forwards into a front stance and drive both open hands upwards and forwards, allowing them to cross at the wrist, with the right wrist resting on the left wrist. The wrists

Fig 125   Shuto Juji Uke.

Fig 126   Shuto Uke.

should be positioned just above and slightly in front of the head. The body must remain upright.

SHUTO UKE

Knife-hand block. Stepping with the left foot forwards in stance, draw the left open hand to the right shoulder with the palm to the face and the left elbow close to the solar plexus. Allow the arm to pivot at the elbow and drive forwards with the thumb edge of the left hand in a diagonal line from right to left until the hand is almost level with the left shoulder, with the palm facing upwards. When this point is reached, allow the hand to flip over so that the palm is now facing downwards and the outer edge, or little finger edge, of the hand makes the strike. Do not allow the elbow to point away from the body; keep the triceps in line with the side of the chest with a gap of about 6in (15cm). While performing this action, draw the right open hand back to the body with the palm facing upwards and the edge of the hand resting on the solar plexus. The hands should be straight, with the fingers pressed together.

SOETE

Supporting. Usually refers to one arm supporting the other: in Fig 127 the left arm is supporting the right

Fig 127   Soete.

SOETE KOSHI GAMAE

Supporting hip posture. The hand positions for this technique are the same as for the Empi posture above.

Fig 128   Soete Koshi Gamae.

SOETE MAE EMPI

Supporting front elbow. This is an elbow strike made by driving the elbow forwards and supported by the left open palm. The elbow and upper forearm are used to make the strike.

SOETE SOKUMEN UKE

Side view supported forearm block. This is a middle-level forearm block made to the side of the body and supported by the opposite open hand palm. The action is one of the open palm sliding down the blocking forearm as it moves across the body.

Fig 129   Soete Mae Empi.

Fig 130   Soete Sokumen Uke.

Fig 131   Soete Urazuki.

Fig 132   Soesho Chudan Zuki.

SOETE URAZUKI

Supported close punch. This is a downward spiralling strike. Raise the right arm above the head and drive downwards and forwards to make a back-fist strike. The right arm is usually supported at the elbow by the back of the left fist.

SOESHO CHUDAN ZUKI

Attached middle-level strike. This is a middle-level strike with the arm supported at the elbow with the opposite open hand.

SOESHO KAESHI UDE

Attached palm hand arm. This is a short hooking movement made here after a forward strike.

Fig 133   Soesho Kaeshi Ude.

SOKUMEN EMPI

Side view elbow strike. This is an elbow strike delivered to the opposite open hand and to the side of the body.

Fig 134   Sokumen Empi.

Fig 135   Sokumen Soete Gedan Uchi Ude Uke.

SOKUMEN SOETE GEDAN UCHI UDE UKE

Side view supported low-level striking arm block. This is a supported low-level forearm block.

SOKUMEN TATE SHUTO UKE

Side view vertical knife hand block. This is an open hand block that scoops around from one side of the body to the other. Here the right hand has been raised to the left shoulder and pushed outwards and around to the right side. Throughout the action the palm of the open hand is directed outwards.

SOKUMEN TETTSUI OTOSHI UCHI

Side view hammer fist dropping strike. Extend the right arm to the right of the body at middle level. Place the left open

Fig 136   Sokumen Tate Shuto Uke.

Fig 137 *Sokumen Tettsui Otoshi Uchi.*

is intended to support the right blocking arm. Alternatively, the supporting fist may rest under the elbow with the elbow touching the back of the hand.

SOKUMEN ZUKI

Side view srike. Here the fist is driven across the chest to make a strike to the side, similar to *Kagi Zuki.*

SOTO UKE

Attached counter arm. This is an inward-winding block and involves driving the arm downwards from a high position to make a middle-level forearm block. The

hand on top of the elbow joint of the right arm, and allow the left thumb to rest under the elbow. Maintaining the left hand position, rotate the right arm in a large clockwise direction, bringing the little finger edge of the right fist downwards to the right side of the body at middle level.

SOKUMEN UKE

Side view block. Raise the right fist to the left shoulder with the back of the fist to the face and the elbow close to the chest. Drive the right fist out to the right of the body until the fist is level with, and in line with, the right shoulder. The arm should be bent at the elbow in a 'V' shape. When this point is reached, allow the fist to turn clockwise until the palm is facing upwards. While performing this action, draw the left fist to the right elbow, to the side and just behind the elbow joint, with the palm of the left fist directed upwards. The left fist

Fig 138 *Sokumen Uke.*

Fig 139   Sokumen Zuki.

Fig 140   Soto Uke.

arm is bent at the elbow in a 'V' shape and the palm of the fist is directed upwards.

SOTO UDE UKE

Attached arm block. This is slightly like a *Gedan Barai* but with the palm of the fist directed upwards and supported at the elbow between the thumb and first finger of the opposite hand.

SOWAN UCHI UKE

Set, pair strike block. The movements for this technique are the same as for *Kakiwake Uke* but with the palms of the fists directed towards the face.

SUKUI UKE

Scooping block. This technique can be

Fig 141   Soto Ude Uke.

Fig 143   Sukui Uke.

Fig 142   Sowan Uchi Uke.

Fig 144   Sukui Uke.

performed in two ways: (i) step to the right into a front stance and look forwards. Draw the left fist to the left hip with the fingers facing upwards. Raise the right arm vertically until it is almost straight. Turn the body slightly to the left and allow the body weight to fall on the left leg. Swing the right arm in a clockwise direction downwards and low across the lower part of the body. As the arm descends, use the thumb edge of the hand to drive forwards until it reaches a point level with the left side of the body. At this point, pivot at the elbow and swing the arm around and upwards until it is level with the left side of the abdomen in an *Ude Uke* position. The armpit should be closed and the elbow about 6in (15cm) away from the right side of the chest; (ii) stand in an informal attention. Bending at the knees, allow the body weight to sink downwards. At the same time, drive the right fist in a anti-clockwise direction across the lower part of the body. Complete a large half anti-clockwise circle with the right arm until it is level with the head, and raise the body.

TACHI HIZA

Stance knee. Step forwards with the left foot into a front stance. Allow the right knee to bend until it rests on the floor. The

Fig 145   Tachi Hiza.

lower part of the right leg should be vertical, and the ball of the left foot should be resting on the floor.

TATE EMPI UCHI

Vertical elbow strike. This is a rising elbow strike. Here the left fist has been driven from the left hip and over the left shoulder so that the elbow is pointing forwards. This is often expressed by striking the opposite open hand.

TATE SHUTO UKE

Vertical knife-hand block. The movement

Fig 146 Tate Empi Uchi.

Fig 146(a) Tate Empi Uchi.

Fig 147   Tate Shuto Uke.

Fig 148   Tate Zuki.

for this technique is the same as for *Sokumen Tate Shuto Uke*, but in this case the open hand is directed out to the front of the body rather than to the side.

TATE ZUKI

Vertical strike. This is a rising punch used here by driving the right fist upwards across the chest to the left shoulder with the palm of the fist facing the left shoulder. The feeling here is one of striking to the face of an attacker to the rear, slightly to the left side of the body.

TEISHO AWASE GEDAN UKE

Palm-heel combined low-level block. Drive downwards with both open hands to a

Fig 149   Teisho Awase Gedan Uke.

low-level blocking position. The palm heels are used to make the block, with the wrists almost touching and the hands held wide apart.

TEISHO KOSA UKE

Palm-heel crossed block. This is a palm-heel block using both hands at the same time. The left open hand is raised to the height of the left shoulder and starts to press down to low level, and the right hand starts at low level and starts to drive upwards.

Fig 150   Teisho Kosa Uke.

TEISHO UKE

Palm-heel block. Draw the right hand to the right hip, and turn the open hand over so the palm is facing forwards and the fingertips pointing downwards. Drive forwards and upwards using the heel of the hand until it is in line with the centre of the body. At this point, the right palm heel should be in line with the sternum.

Fig 151 Teisho Uke.

TEISHO UCHI

Palm-heel strike. The action for this technique is similar to *Teisho Uke* but the palm heel is driven out to the side of the body in a striking action.

TEISHO MOROTE UKE

Palm-heel two hands block. This is a palm-heel block using both hands at the same time. The left open hand is raised to the

Fig 152   Teisho Uke.

Fig 153   Teisho Morote Uke.

height of the left shoulder and starts to press down to low level, and the right hand starts at low level and starts to drive upwards.

TEKKI SHODAN POSTURE

Stand with the feet together and the knees slightly bent. The back must remain straight and the posterior pushed in. The hands are brought together just in front of the groin, with the left palm resting on the back of the right hand, and both palms facing downwards. The right fingers are pointing diagonally to the left and the left fingers diagonally to the right, forming a cross. The arms are slightly bent at the elbows, the armpits are closed and the thumb edge of each hand is about 4in (10cm) from the groin. The shoulders are relaxed.

TEKUBI KAKE UKE

Wrist hook block. Raise the right fist to the left shoulder with the back of the fist to the face and the elbow close to the chest. While opening the hand, drive forwards in a diagonal line from left to right until the open hand is level with the right shoulder. The arm should be bent at the elbow in a 'V' shape. When this point is reached, the back of the hand should be directed downwards, the fingers pointing forwards. The back of the wrist is used to make the block.

TETTSUI UCHI

Hammer-fist strike. Raise the right fist to the left shoulder with the fingers to the right side of the face. Allow the upper body to turn slightly to the left. Drive the back of the fist forward in an arc and out

Fig 154   Tekubi Kake Uke.

Fig 155   Tettsui Uchi.

to the right side of the body to middle level. When the arm is almost extended, allow the fist to turn clockwise, so the little finger edge of the fist is facing to the rear.

TETTSUI HASAMI UCHI

Hammer-fist scissors strike. Position both arms out to either side of the body in line with the hips with the fingers directed downwards. Drive forwards in an arc until the fists are extended in front of the chest about 6in (15cm) apart. At this point, allow the fists to turn, so the little finger edges are directed towards each other.

Fig 156   Tettsui Hasami Uchi.

Fig 157   Tettsui Otoshi Uchi

Fig 157 (a)   Tettsui Otoshi Uchi.

TETTSUI OTOSHI UCHI

Hammer-fist dropping strike. Extend the right arm out to the right side of the body at low level. Rotate the right arm in a full, large clockwise circle, and bring the little finger edge of the fist down to make the strike.

TOBI GERI

Jumping kick. See Fig 84, *Mae Tobi Geri.* This involves jumping several feet into the air to make a kicking action, in this case a front kick.

TSUKAMI UKE

Grasping block. Reach across with the

Fig 158   Tsukami Uke.

Fig 159   Tsuru Ashi Dachi.

right open hand to the left side of the body. The palm should be facing downwards and the fingers pressed together, as if grasping the arm or sleeve of an attacker approaching from the left side.

TSURU ASHI DACHI

Crane-leg stance. Standing on the left foot, raise the right foot upwards and behind the left knee. The left leg should be slightly bent, and the top of the right foot should be resting in the arch behind the left knee.

UDE SOETE

Supporting block. Step with the left foot into a back stance. Raise the right fist to the right temple area of the head, with the back of the hand touching the temple, and the elbow angled away from the body.

Fig 160   Ude Soete.

UCHI UDE UKE

Striking arm block. The action for this technique is the same as for *Uchi Uke* but with the opposite open hand supporting the lower inner forearm.

UCHI UKE

Striking block. Raise the right fist to the left shoulder with the back of the fist to the face and the elbow close to the chest. Drive forwards in a diagonal line from left to right until the fist is level with the right shoulder and in line with the right knee. The arm should be bent at the elbow in a 'V' shape. When this point is reached, allow the fist to turn clockwise until the palm is facing upwards.

URAZUKI

Close punch. This is a punch usually made in close proximity to the attacker. In this example the strike is made using the right fist to punch upwards into the solar plexus.

Fig 161   Uchi Ude Uke.

Fig 162   Uchi Uke.

Fig 163   Urasuki.

URAKEN UCHI

Back fist. This is often used in combination with *Yoko Geri Keage*. Drive out to the side with the back of the fist and, when the arm is extended at head height, allow the wrist to flex. The arm and wrist should make a whipping action as the strike is made – a fast recoiling action, with the knuckles making contact rather than the back of the hand.

USHIRO GEDAN BARAI

Rear low-level sweeping. Step with the

Fig 164   Uraken Uchi.

right leg into a front stance. Draw the right fist to the right hip with the fingers facing upwards. Draw the left fist to the right shoulder with the fingers towards the face. Allowing the body to turn to the left, look over the left shoulder. Drive downwards with the left fist, in a low-level block, until

147

Fig 165   Ushiro Gedan Barai.

Fig 166   Yama Kakiwake.

it reaches a point about 6in (15cm) above the left thigh. Allow the right fist to turn clockwise at the end of the low-level block.

YAMA KAKIWAKE

Mountain wedging. Both arms are raised to the side with the palms facing outwards, The forearms are used to make the blocks. In some situations this technique is referred to as *Yama Uke*, and the fists may be turned so the palms are facing the sies of the head.

YAMA ZUKI

Mountain punch. Step with the left foot into a front stance. Drive the left arm forwards to make a middle-level punch and, at the same time, drive the right fist over the head to make a high-level punch. At the end of this strike the fists should be in vertical alignment.

YOI

Ready stance. Stand with the feet shoulder-

Fig 167   Yama Uke.

Fig 168   Yama Zuki.

width apart and the toes pointing forwards. The fists are closed with a loose gripping action. The whole body is relaxed and the arms are resting in a natural position at the sides of the body. This is the basic stance and the one most commonly used.

YOKO GERI KEAGE

Side kick snapping. Raise the right foot to the height of the left knee, and drive the right foot out to the side to about waist height, driving with the hips. The outer edge of the right foot should make contact.

YOKO SASHI ASHI

Side balance leg. This is a stepping action of one foot over the other; a strong sense of balance is required.

149

Fig 169 Yoi.

YOKO UDE HASAMI

Side arm scissors. Take the left arm with closed fist to the position of a low-level block. Raise the right arm to the right side of the head so that the upper arm is horizontal to the right shoulder and the fore-arm is vertically aligned, in an 'L' shape. Drive both arms towards each other until

Fig 170   Yoko Sashi Ashi.

Fig 171   Yoko Geri Keage

150

they are parallel to each other across the chest. The back of the left hand should be touching the upper right forearm and the little finger edge of the right arm should be touching the upper left forearm.

YORI ASHI

Sliding foot. This is simply a little sliding movement and may be performed in any stance. For this example, step into a horse-riding stance and, by lifting the weight off the right foot, slide to the right about 5 or

Fig 172   Yoko Ude Hasami

6in (12-15cm), then allow the left foot to move in the same direction equally.

YUMI ZUKI

Bow strike. The action for this technique is rather like using a bow, pulling back with the left arm and driving out to the side with the right arm.

Fig 173   Yori Ashi.

ZENKUTSU DACHI

Front bent leg stance. See Fig 23 for positioning the feet. Front stance is rather like taking a long step forwards, but with a few simple guidelines. Before making the step forwards, gauge the width of the shoulders from left to right. Using that measurement, imagine two equal parallel lines on the floor having that same shoulder-width distance between them. Place the left foot on the left line and the right foot on the right line. Step along the left

Fig 174   Yumi Zuki.

Fig 175   Zenkutsu Dachi.

line with the left foot as far as you can without wobbling or falling and keep the body facing forwards. Allow the right foot to turn 35 degrees to the right and keep the left foot pointing forwards. Keeping the feet firmly in place, move the body weight forward by bending the left knee until it is vertically level with the toes. Keep the sole of the right foot firmly planted on the floor and do not allow it to roll on to the inner edge. Keep the body upright.

Appendix

SAMPLE GRADING SYLLABUS

Student's Name: —————————————

Current Grade: —————————————

- Candidates must have a good attendance record prior to the grading.
- Membership must be up to date, and grading fee paid in advance.
- The syllabus has five levels of grading relating to performance:-

  - Grade 1: Kata and techniques at beginner level ——
  - Grade 2: Practice and familiarity with 'form' ——
  - Grade 3: Good execution of techniques ——
  - Grade 4: Understanding of interpretation and application ——
  - Gade 5: Excellent performance / good mental attitude ——

- From 6th Kyu to 1st Kyu each candidate must achieve a minimum of Grade 3.
- Dan grade candidates must achieve Grade 5 in all requested activities.

  A variety of other activities are required at different levels.
  A demonstration of a number of kata are also required, e.g. :-

- 6th Kyu - White Belt:
  Taikyoku Shodan, Taikyoku Nidan, Taikyoku Sandan.
- 5th Kyu - Yellow Belt:
  As above plus Heian Shodan, Heian Nidan.
- 4th Kyu - Orange Belt:
  As above plus Heian Sandan, Heian Yodan.
- 3rd Kyu - Green Belt:
  As above plus Heian Godan.
- 2nd Kyu - Blue Belt:
  As above plus Tekki Shodan, Tekki Nidan, Tekki Sandan.
- 1st Kyu - Brown Belt:
  As above plus Bassai Dai

Grade Awarded: —————————————

Date Grade Awarded: —————————————

Grading Offer's Signature: —————————————

Dan Grade candidates are often asked to submit a short essay about Karate to demonstrate understanding.

Bibliography

upright.

Layton, Dr Clive, *Mysteries of the Martial Arts* (Kima Publishing, Huntington, 1989, ISBN 0-9513406-1-1)

Layton, Dr Clive, *Conversations with Karate Masters* (Ronin Publishing, 1988) (publishers of Fighting Arts International, Birkenhead, ISBN 1-871457-00-9)

Hyams, Joe, *Zen in the Martial Arts* (J.P. Tarcher Inc., Los Angeles, 1979, distributed by St Martin's Press, New York, ISBN 0-87477-114-5 [cloth], 0-87177-101-3 [paper])

Lovatt, John, *Japanese-English Dictionary* (unpublished, presented 1978 to the International Martial Arts Federation as part of the qualifying procedure for the title of Renshi)

Master Gichin Funakoshi, *Karate-do Kyohan, The Master Text* (2nd edition)

Master Gichin Funakoshi, *Karate-do, My Way of Life* (Kodansha International Ltd, 1975, ISBN 0-87011-463-8)

Master Gichin Funakoshi, Johm Teramotob (trans.), *Karate-do Nyumon,* The Master Text (Kodansha International, 1988, ISBN 0-87011-819-6)

Master Morihei Ueshiba, a quote from one of the Master's scrolls
Shigeru Egami, *The Heart of Karate-do* (Harper and Row, 1976, ISBN 0-87011-437-9)

The Oxford Illustrated Dictionary (Oxford University Press)

Index